Ageing Europe

ALAN WALKER
and
TONY MALTBY

OPEN UNIVERSITY PRESS
Buckingham · Philadelphia

To Alison, Christopher and Joanne

Open University Press
Celtic Court
22 Ballmoor
Buckingham
MK18 1XW

and

1900 Frost Road, Suite 101
Bristol, PA 19007, USA

First Published 1997

Copyright © Alan Walker and Tony Maltby 1997

A catalogue record of this book is available from the British Library

ISBN 0 335 19746 9 (pbk)   0 335 19747 7 (hbk)

Library of Congress Cataloging-in-Publication Data

Walker, Alan.
    Ageing Europe / Alan Walker and Tony Maltby.
        p.   cm. — (Rethinking ageing series)
    Includes bibliographical references and index.
    ISBN 0–335–19746–9 (pbk.)   ISBN 0–335–19747–7 (hbk)
    1. Ageing — Social aspects — European Union countries.   2. Aged — European Union countries — Social conditions.   3. Old age — European Union countries.   I. Maltby, Tony.   II. Title.   III. Series.
HQ1064.E87W35   1996
305.26'094—dc20   96–9095
                                                                                                          CIP

Typeset by Type Study, Scarborough
Printed in Great Britain by Biddles Limited, Guildford and Kings Lynn

Ageing Europe

RETHINKING AGEING SERIES

Series editor: Brian Gearing
                School of Health and Social Welfare
                The Open University

The rapid growth in ageing populations in Britain and other countries has led to a dramatic increase in academic and professional interest in the subject. Over the past decade this has led to the publication of many research studies which have stimulated new ideas and fresh approaches to understanding old age. At the same time, there has been concern about continued neglect of ageing and old age in the education and professional training of most workers in health and social services, and about inadequate dissemination of the new information and ideas about ageing to a wider public.

This series aims to fill a gap in the market for accessible, up-to-date studies of important issues in ageing. Each book will focus on a topic of current concern addressing two fundamental questions: what is known about this topic? And what are the policy, service and practice implications of our knowledge? Authors will be encouraged to develop their own ideas, drawing on case material, and their own research, professional or personal experience. The books will be interdisciplinary, and written in clear, non-technical language which will appeal to a broad range of students, academics and professionals with a common interest in ageing and age care.

Current and forthcoming titles:
Simon Biggs *et al*.: **Elder abuse in perspective**
Ken Blakemore and Margaret Boneham: **Age, race and ethnicity:
    A comparative approach**
Joanna Bornat (ed.): **Reminiscence reviewed: Evaluations,
    achievements, perspectives**
Joanna Bornat and Maureen Cooper: **Older learners**
Bill Bytheway: **Ageism**
Beverley Hughes: **Older people and community care**
Anne Jamieson: **Comparing policies of care for older people**
Sheila Peace *et al*.: **Re-evaluating residential care**
Moyra Sidell: **Health in old age: Myth, mystery and management**
Andrew Sixsmith: **Quality of life: Rethinking well-being in old age**
Robert Slater: **The psychology of growing old: Looking forward**
Alan Walker and Tony Maltby: **Ageing Europe**
Eric Midwinter: **Pensioned off**

Contents

Series editor's preface

Ageing Europe is a major contribution to the 'Rethinking Ageing' series and to ageing studies, being the first book to make available to a wide audience the results of the research in 12 European countries which was carried out under the European Union's first Programme of Actions on the Elderly. It therefore makes international comparisons possible for the first time. Alan Walker was the UK's national scientific expert and a member of the Observatory on Ageing and Older People, which was created in 1991 to monitor the impact of social and economic policies on older people within each member state. The uniquely broad and detailed coverage of topics and EU countries produced by the Observatory gives the most comprehensive picture available so far of the living conditions and other social, economic and health circumstances of Europe's older citizens. Data were also collected about the attitudes of older people towards ageing and, via the Eurobarometer survey, of the general public towards them. In *Ageing Europe*, Alan Walker and Tony Maltby draw on all of that information to present uniquely the first comprehensive picture of the position of older people in the countries of the European Union. They also analyse the most important policy issues confronting ageing societies in Europe in the light of this research.

Walker and Maltby's book fills a gap in the 'Rethinking Ageing' series, in being the first book in the series to be concerned mainly with economic and social policy. Readers of the book who are particularly interested in the wellbeing of older people in Britain will find that it presents an analysis of the position of older UK citizens based on the latest information about living standards, employment position, health and social care, community care and political activity. It also focuses on topical issues like long-term care. This illuminating review is strengthened by being seen in the perspective of the circumstances of older people in other European societies.

There are grounds for both optimism and pessimism coming from the

European research presented in this book. On the negative side, it underlines the existence of serious social problems affecting very many older people, including the persistence of poverty and low levels of pensions in some countries such as the UK. There is also a high level of pessimism among the general public in all EU countries about how far the pensions contract between government and governed will be honoured, and a widespread pessimism about the future of welfare states. The growing numbers of older people who are living alone and at risk of isolation (particularly women) are grounds for serious concern, as is the existence of widespread age discrimination in employment.

However, grounds for optimism include the extent to which older people remain integrated with family and neighbourhood throughout Europe. There is confirmation that many older people provide care as volunteers or family members. And contrary to the recent soundings of alarm on this topic, there is evidence of intergenerational solidarity between workers and pensioners. Indeed, the general public expressed heartening views on the undesirability of people over 50 years of age having to make way for the young in the labour force. What is more, only a small proportion of Europe's older citizens thought they had been treated as second-class citizens. Of course, much still needs to be done to raise the living standards of older people throughout Europe to the level enjoyed by those pensioners in a minority of EU states, and to remove barriers to the full social integration of those older people who have yet to achieve full citizenship. As this research shows, however, governments underestimate the extent to which the general population might support policies aimed at securing the wellbeing of older people. The authors put forward a strategy for this in the final chapter, focusing on four key areas, a strategy one hopes will be noted by policy makers (and be subject to political action by older people themselves).

In being based on the European research studies, this book departs from the established topic-based format of the series. At the same time, by *rethinking* policies based on its presentation and analyses of data not previously available on such a comprehensive scale, *Ageing Europe* admirably fulfils the overall purpose of the series, which is to contribute to a rethinking of ageing and the position of older people in society. And at a time when myths, prejudice and ignorance about older people still exist, it provides a sound basis for realistic policy making.

Brian Gearing
School of Health and Social Welfare
The Open University

Acknowledgements

Because this book relies heavily on a body of research – primary data collection and secondary analyses – that I was responsible for under the European Union's first Programme of Actions on the Elderly, Tony Maltby has graciously allowed me to use these acknowledgements to thank my various collaborators in these ventures.

As head of the Commission's section responsible for the programme, Éamon McInerney deserves special thanks for his constant support and enthusiastic collaboration in all of the work I undertook. When the histories are written of European social policy and of the growth of European social movements of older people, Éamon McInerney should occupy a prominent place for his inspired stewardship of the actions programme. Odile Quintin, the head of DGV C/1 at the time, also deserves considerable credit both for the establishment of the Observatory and for conceiving the idea of the Eurobarometer study. She was also responsible for approving the Observatory's research agenda and facilitated several meetings of the network. It was a privilege to work closely with two such outstanding officials and to share with them a vision of European social policy.

As will be clear from the Introduction, the Observatory was a collaborative venture and, although there were initially three coordinators and later one chair, all aspects of the research programme were discussed at meetings of the full Observatory and the European syntheses were based on national reports prepared by individual experts. Thus sincere thanks are due to my Observatory collaborators: Jens Alber, Juan Antonio Fernandez Cordon, Aurelia Florea, Anne-Marie Guillemard, Kees Knipscheer, Olgierd Kuty, Éamon O'Shea, Heloisa Perista, Merete Platz, Gaston Shaber and Dimitris Ziomas. Jens Alber and Anne-Marie Guillemard were the joint coordinators of the Observatory and played important roles in establishing the research agenda and guidelines for national experts. Anne-Marie's continuous collaboration and intellectual inspiration are appreciated deeply.

It was of considerable embarrassment that, when the initial report on the 1992 Eurobarometer survey was published (Walker 1993a), I was not permitted to include any acknowledgements. That deficiency can be rectified now. As well as the support of DGV, I would also like to thank Dominque Vancraeynest and his colleagues at INRA (Europe), who skilfully organized the field work, data preparation and production of tables. In a public opinion survey such as the Eurobarometer, the vital research tool is the questionnaire, and various people made helpful comments on successive drafts: Karen Chapman, Bettina Knauth, Éamon McInerney, Chris Phillipson, Lee Rainwater, Dominque Vancraeynest, John Westergaard and members of the Observatory on Ageing and Older People, especially Jens Alber, Gaston Schaber and Heloisa Perista. Special thanks are due to Bettina Knauth and her colleagues at Eurostat, who organized a small-scale pilot test of one of the draft questionnaires. (Also, Eurostat have kindly agreed to the publication of Figures 2.1 and 2.2.) Eric Midwinter's pioneering work on the British Gas survey of attitudes to ageing in Britain provided an important reference point for the Eurobarometer survey.

Last, but not least in terms of gratitude, throughout all of this European research and in the completion of this book the highest standards of secretarial and technical assistance have been provided by Marilyn Shipley and Marg Walker.

Tony and I dedicate the book to our children – Alison, Christopher and Joanne – in the hope that Europe will have come fully to terms with the ageing of its population by the time they are classified by social scientists as older people.

Alan Walker
Department of Sociological Studies
University of Sheffield

1

Introduction

At the turn of the century in an imaginary average European city one would have expected to encounter one person aged 65 or over among every 20 people; in 1996 it would be one in every seven and by 2020 it will be one in every five. Moreover, today those aged 75 and over comprise one in 15 persons, while by 2020 it will be nearly one in ten. While it is becoming commonplace to observe that Europe is ageing fast and while there is ample political rhetoric concerning the 'burdens' of an ageing population (Walker 1990), before the research reported here there had not been any detailed studies across the European Union (EU)[1] of the impact on national policies of this momentous change. Nor had there been any previous European surveys of public attitudes to ageing and older people.

The main purpose of this book, therefore, is to make available to a wide readership the results of some unique research carried out under the EU's first Programme of Actions for the Elderly. These data on older people in Europe were derived from two main sources: the secondary analyses conducted by the EU Observatory on Ageing and Older People and the special Eurobarometer survey initiated as part of the Commission's preparations for the European Year of Older People and Solidarity Between the Generations (1993). In this introductory chapter we explain the background to these research studies and, first of all, the role of observatories in policy making at a European level.

The European observatories

As far as we can ascertain, the concept of observatories is a uniquely European one. They were first created in France, following the administrative decentralization to the regions in the 1980s, with the intention of monitoring local developments in order to contribute to coherence in national policy making (Room *et al.* 1992: 13). Their European forebears were the Mutual Information System on Employment Policies (MISEP), a network of national government experts set up in 1982 to gather, synthesize and disseminate information on employment policies, and the various research groups established to monitor the impact of Community legislation, for example in the field of equal opportunities between men and women.

In the late 1980s and early 1990s this information gathering, synthesizing and dissemination was expanded considerably by the establishment of observatories consisting of networks of independent experts in each member state. The first was the Observatory on National Family Policies, set up in 1989. This was followed, in 1990, by the Observatory on National Policies to Combat Social Exclusion, the Mutual Information System on Social Protection in the Member States of the Community (Missoc), and the European System of Documentation on Employment (SYSDEM). (Together with MISEP, a network of officials from the employment administrations of the member states and regular reviews of employment issues in Central and Eastern Europe, SYSDEM comprises the European Observatory on Employment.) In 1991, as instructed by a decision of the Council of Ministers on 26 November 1990, the Observatory on Ageing and Older People was formed. Finally, in 1992, an observatory was created, as part of the implementation of the Social Charter, to monitor complementary pension systems (Quintin 1993). In addition to these five observatories and Missoc there is a European Observatory on Homelessness, which is supported by the Commission but which operates entirely independently of it (Daly 1993).

Although there are variations in operation between observatories, the pattern is broadly similar. The national experts, one from each member state, prepare annual reports based on guidelines set out and agreed by the observatory as a whole in consultation with the Commission. These reports are then synthesized and a summary report of the main trends is prepared by the coordinator or chair of the observatory. In addition, and again in close consultation with the Commission, an observatory may prepare special reports on designated topics. For example, in 1993, the Observatory on Social Exclusion prepared a special report on social services and the Observatory on Ageing and Older People produced one on social integration. Observatory members meet together three or four times a year.

There are frequent misunderstandings about the role and functions of observatories. They consist of independent scientific experts whose task it is to monitor and analyse national policy developments and to report on overall trends and new policy initiatives in the Union. Their guiding principles are those of independence and impartiality. However, monitoring and evaluation necessarily entail the drawing of conclusions, either implicitly or explicitly. The audience addressed by the observatories includes the Commission, the European Parliament, national and regional policy makers, the representatives of various interests, including the social partners and non-governmental organizations (NGOs), the European media and the general public. Observatories are not responsible for the dissemination of their results – that is a matter for the Commission.

The role of observatories in the convergence of social policy

Observatories may be regarded as important facilitators of convergence of social policies within the EU. The work they undertake is likely to assist convergence in four ways.

First, the observatories support the European Commission's role with regard to convergence by highlighting differences and similarities in responses to the common social issues that member states are facing, such as population ageing and isolation among some older people, the growth in the numbers of single-parent families, increasing homelessness, the relationship between social assistance and the labour market, and so on. On the basis of the observatory reports, the Commission is better placed to encourage a transfer of knowledge about social policy and practice between the member states.

Secondly, there is the demonstration effect. Observatories are inevitably highlighting both good and bad practice and, as they move beyond monitoring and undertake more policy evaluation, this demonstration effect will heighten as it encourages national policy makers to assess their interventions in the light of practice elsewhere in the EU.

Following on from this, thirdly, the work of the observatories may encourage national and regional policy makers to investigate in greater depth policy models or approaches adopted in another member state and this could contribute to more extensive comparative research and improvements in the quality of national statistics. As all observatory members know, there is huge variation in the quality of the social statistics provided by the member states. Since knowledge is a fundamental requisite for convergence, the well known inadequacies of Europe's comparative statistics are themselves a barrier to its achievement.

Fourthly, observatory reports are aimed not only at European and national policy makers but also the wider policy arena, especially NGOs. Thus by improving the information available to different national and trans-national groups, observatories are enhancing the role of these groups in encouraging convergence between member states.

The EU's Observatory on Ageing and Older People

The Observatory on Ageing and Older People was created to monitor the impact of social and economic policies on older people within each member state. By doing so it was intended to assist the Commission in sharing knowledge between countries about the impact of different policies on older people and to create an EU-wide picture of the social and economic conditions of this group of citizens. Thus, in the spirit of the subsidiarity principle, the work of the Observatory was strictly confined to areas that are beyond the scope of national action alone. Essentially its role was to help the Commission to gain 'added value' from Community membership for the then 12 member states. By obtaining authoritative reports from each country, synthesizing their findings and disseminating them widely, the Observatory set out to contribute to the development of policies on older people in the member states, as well as to the level and quality of the information each has about policy and practice in the other 11. There is no doubt too that this observatory, like the others, was intended to contribute to the convergence of national policies.

The Observatory was established at the beginning of 1991 following a decision by the EC Council of Ministers on 26 November 1990 (91/49/EEC) to institute the Programme of Actions for the Elderly. Thus, uniquely, the Observatory on Ageing and Older People was mandated by a Council decision. There were four main factors underlying the creation of the Observatory: the significant demographic changes over the 33 years since the Treaty of Rome in 1957; the general desire to promote solidarity between generations and to integrate older people more fully into society; the demands for action with regard to older people by the European Parliament; and the various commitments concerning this group given in the Social Charter (especially paragraphs 24 and 25). The Observatory formed part of a wider programme of actions, running from 1 January 1991 to 31 December 1993, including information exchanges, meetings, seminars and conferences; a network of innovatory projects; cross-national research studies; and the designation of 1993 as the European Year of Older People and Solidarity Between the Generations. Its role in the context of this action programme was the scientific monitoring of the impact of social and economic policies on older people. The budget for the European Year was 7.5 million ECU (£5.3 million) and more than 1000 meetings and events were held under the auspices of the EU (see pp. 117–20).

Research agenda of the Observatory

The Council decision of November 1990 specifically charged the Commission with monitoring and exchanging information concerning demographic trends and their impact on social protection and health systems; measures aimed at improving the mobility of older people and their ability to lead an independent life; measures to strengthen solidarity between generations and promote the positive contribution of older people to economic and social life; and the economic and social integration of older people, including their income.

In discussions with the Commission it was decided that, to fulfil the objectives laid down for the Observatory, its research and monitoring activity should be concentrated on four specific topics:

1 living standards and way of life;
2 employment and the labour market;
3 health and social care;
4 the social integration of older people in both formal and informal settings.

These were the four subject areas covered in the preliminary report published in 1991 (Walker *et al.* 1991). During the European Year of Older People and Solidarity Between the Generations, the Observatory produced two reports: *Older People in Europe: Social and Economic Policies* (Walker *et al.* 1993) and *Older People in Europe: Social Integration* (Walker 1993b). Both reports were listed in the Council decision of 24 June 1992 as key elements of the publication programme for the European Year. The objectives of the year were set out in that Council decision:

- to highlight the Community's social dimension;
- to heighten society's awareness of the situation of older people, the challenges resulting from present and future demographic developments and the consequences of an ageing population for all Community policies;
- to promote reflection and discussion on the types of change required in order to deal with this situation and these developments;
- to promote the principle of solidarity between generations;
- to involve older people more in the process of Community integration.

Organization of the Observatory

The Observatory comprised a network of 12 independent scientific experts, one from each member state. They collected and analysed extant national data, including official statistics, policy documents, legislation, and parliamentary reports, following guidelines established by the coordinators – Jens Alber, Anne-Marie Guillemard, and Alan Walker as chair – and developed in discussions of the full Observatory. The coordinators were then responsible for synthesizing the information contained in the national reports and preparing an overview. European overviews produced by observatories are not intended to be reviews of current research; they are derived almost entirely from the reports produced by the national experts which, in turn, are meant to be 'state of the art' summaries of the key policy issues in each member state.

The Observatory on Ageing and Older People was a genuinely collaborative venture linking all of the then 12 member states. Its research output was unique – there had been no similar venture in this field so comprehensive in its coverage of topics and EU countries. The national reports represented important sources of reference for further research – only a flavour of which can be gained from the overviews – and accordingly they were published at the same time as the European reports. (The names of the Observatory members can be found in Appendix I.) These reports are warmly recommended to anyone with an interest in the detailed information on the living conditions, employment and health and social care of older people in the separate member states. Together this body of work represents the most comprehensive picture available so far of the social and economic conditions of older citizens in the different EU countries.

Because the Observatory was established as part of the EU's Programme of Actions for the Elderly its timetable was determined by the needs of the wider programme. In particular the Observatory had to be set up and its first report delivered within only six months. This enormous haste entailed the loss of one country (Italy) and the preparation of a brief and rather superficial preliminary report. Although the next phase of the Observatory work was geared towards the European Year, the timetable was more relaxed and not only was there a full complement of countries, but also the research carried out by national experts was considerably more detailed.

Methodology

The Observatory was charged with analysing the impact of social and economic policies on older people. To make this broad remit more manageable it was delineated into the four topics outlined above. Obviously this was still a massive field to cover on a comparative basis across 12 countries. It would be a difficult task even if the national statistical and administrative information systems in each member state were aligned, but unfortunately they are not. Thus the Observatory, like any similarly large-scale comparative venture, faced the enormous barrier of the incomparability of many national data sets. This problem was compounded by the rudimentary nature of the statistics available in some countries. Therefore in some cases the Observatory experts were forced to rely on aggregate EU data and in others there was no alternative but to exclude certain countries. This was a particular problem with regard to data on living standards, and virtually every national report on social and economic policies draws attention to the lack of detailed information in this area and the absence of up-to-date figures. This widespread deficiency in official statistics and independent research evidence about the living standards of older people has important policy implications, not the least of which is that policy makers lack an adequate basis on which to determine priorities with regard to older people.

As well as consistently criticizing the paucity of comparative and national data on older people, the Observatory's experts also called for more socially oriented and descriptive statistical information. The main presentational gap in many government statistical data is that there is a tendency to describe age ranges in terms of those 'below pensionable age' (where there is considerable differentiation in the age range) and then those above it, with the age group 75 plus being placed in a third category. More differentiation of the age range is required. The reason for this is the great heterogeneity within the older population. Greater differentiation of the statistical data would allow for the more informed analysis of the social and economic indicators they present. As a step towards more sensitive statistical data it should be routine to describe the ranges 50–60, 61–5, 66–75, 76–80 and over 80.

There is also a widespread use of the 'pensioner unit' to denote pensioner households when reporting income. As the use of this term largely reflects male pensioner incomes, it often tends to misrepresent and obscure the generally lower levels of female pensioner income. However, this may be too politically sensitive to change. Similarly there is a need to reinstate the publication of official statistics showing the numbers living below or just above the social assistance levels in each EU country, which may again prove politically sensitive. We address such deficiencies in official statistical series in greater detail in Chapter 4.

The detailed guidelines for the preparation of the Observatory's national reports specified those issues on which national statistical data should be used and those where smaller-scale survey research would be appropriate. But it was not always possible for national experts to maintain this distinction. The bottom line was that if reliable (i.e. scientifically valid) information was available it should be included.

For the most part the national reports were concerned with the aggregate national picture but, in some cases, such as Belgium, Germany, Italy and the UK, it was necessary to point to internal differences between regions. Where there are such differences in the social and economic circumstances of older people within countries these were discussed and the rural/urban distinction figured particularly prominently.

The term 'policy' is central to the Observatory's work, but it is by no means unambiguous. In the literature on social policy it is often applied exclusively to the public sector. There are problems associated with this narrow focus (Walker 1981). In particular it has the effect of obscuring institutions and groups whose policies may be just as significant as those of the state. In this field, for example, occupational pensions and the voluntary or private care sectors may be as important as public provision. Therefore, although much of what was discussed in the Observatory reports related to the policies of national and regional governments, these are not our sole concern. The main focus was on those social and economic policies that have an impact on older people, regardless of the sector from which they originate.

Future of the Observatory

As this general background indicates, the Observatory on Ageing and Older People was in the very early stages of development and had only just begun the complex task of assessing systematically the impact of member states' social and economic policies on older people, just as the Commission itself has only just begun the process of placing the issue of ageing on its policy agenda. Unfortunately, however, the end of the European Year marked the end of the first Programme of Actions. A second programme was due to commence at the beginning of 1996 but, at the time of writing, its future looks very doubtful. The Commission's proposal (Appendix II) is supported by the European Parliament but has not been considered by the Council of Ministers following the German government's rejection of a package containing both the proposal for a decision on EU support for actions in favour of older people and the much larger proposal for a new poverty programme. It would be a great loss to European social policy making if the comparative work of the Observatory does not continue in the same careful and comprehensive way that it started. Its output has been widely acclaimed across the European policy spectrum, from members of the European Parliament to local pensioner action groups. Thus the foundations have been laid for the most extensive and detailed comparative analysis of the impact of social and economic policies on older people available anywhere in the world.

The Eurobarometer survey

As well as drawing on the work of the EU Observatory on Ageing and Older People, this book makes extensive use of data derived from the surveys of European public opinion carried out regularly in each of the member states. In fact the Eurobarometer itself reached adulthood in the autumn of 1991. For the previous 18 years the Commission of the European Communities, through DGX, the Directorate-General for Information, Communication and Culture, has organized a twice-yearly survey covering each of the member states. The twin surveys reported here represented the thirty-seventh in the series and were conducted between 20 April and 18 May 1992. The first was a 'standard'

Eurobarometer survey of the population aged 15 years and over in each of the member states of the EU. The second was a special survey of the population aged 60 and over. The technical specifications for these surveys are contained in Appendix III. The surveys were conducted shortly after the unification of Germany. This provided a unique opportunity to compare the attitudes of the citizens of the former German Democratic Republic (GDR) with those of the old Federal Republic of Germany (FRG). We make reference to any significant differences; otherwise the data are aggregated for the unified Germany.

Although it was the first European survey of public attitudes towards ageing and older people, the Eurobarometer survey was not the only such survey conducted within the then European Community. As a contribution to the European Year, a survey was undertaken by Age Concern (Scotland), the Scottish Consumer Council, and the Senior Studies Institute of the University of Strathclyde, which provided a picture of the problems and difficulties experienced by older people in Scotland (Fell and Foster 1994). Also before the European Year, in May and June 1991, a similar attitudinal survey sponsored by British Gas was conducted by NOP Social and Political, with a commentary by Eric Midwinter (Midwinter 1991). In the following chapters reference is sometimes made to these surveys since they corroborate the findings of the much larger Eurobarometer survey. In addition, the Eurobarometer survey is being replicated, in part or in whole, in various countries, from Australia to Sweden (Anderson 1993; Howe 1993), and therefore we will soon have the basis for even more broadly based international comparisons.

Plan of the book

Over the next six chapters we draw on the information gathered by the Observatory and Eurobarometer to provide as comprehensive a picture as possible of the position of older people in the EU: their social and economic status and their attitudes towards ageing. The data presented usually refer to the EU before the entry of Austria, Sweden and Finland, since the surveys and research upon which this analysis is based were conducted before 1995. However, where possible we have included data which present the position in all 15 EU states. We use the available data to summarize the attitudes of the general public to older people and the most important policy issues confronting ageing societies: intergenerational relations; pensions and living standards; an ageing workforce; the provision of health and social care; and the changing politics of old age. We start with a profile of older Europeans.

Note

1 The EU was established on 1 November 1993, when the 12 member states of the European Community ratified the Maastricht Treaty. As this study spans this period, the term EU is generally used in this book, for convenience. Austria, Sweden and Finland joined the EU in 1995.

2

A profile of older Europeans

Introduction

This chapter begins by providing a brief demographic profile of older people in the EU. This is followed by a descriptive analysis of the attitudes of older people themselves to their position in European society, obtained from the Eurobarometer surveys.

It has been noted by a number of commentators that the adverse effects of social policies on older people often result in the dominant values towards them remaining age discriminatory or ageist – that is, 'the systematic stereotyping of and discrimination against people just because they are old' (Lewis and Butler 1972). The final report of the wide-ranging and important British-based study, the Carnegie Inquiry into the Third Age (henceforth Carnegie Inquiry) (Carnegie Institute 1993), identified this as a common theme running through the results of the nine detailed studies they commissioned as a contribution to the European Year of Older People and Solidarity Between the Generations. This undertone of ageism often condones the perception of older people as a homogeneous entity. For example, press reports in the UK recently suggested that two people over 65 had been refused, respectively, occupational therapy and treatment for a heart condition in two National Health Service (NHS) hospitals simply because they were 'too old'. This assumption of homogeneity is also apparent in many national and European policy documents.

However, what is apparent from the studies conducted during 1993 by the European Observatory on Ageing and Older People, is that older people should *not* be considered as a homogeneous group. Distinguishable differentiation exists among older people as a result of a combination of sociological and other factors such as class (socio-economic position), gender, financial situation and, accompanying these, increasing age.

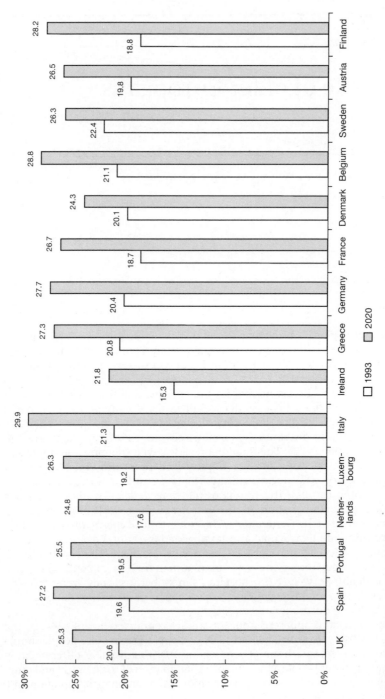

Figure 2.1 Percentage of the population aged 60 and over in the EU countries, 1993 and 2020.
Source: Eurostat, *Demographic Statistics*, 1995 Tables B4, p. 17 and I7, p. 192. Luxembourg: Eurostat.

The demographic context

It is quite clear from demographic data that the EU is an ageing community, yet the rate at which the member states are ageing differs. Ireland has the youngest population of all EU countries and Sweden the oldest, followed by Germany, France and then the UK. The latest available figures from Eurostat indicate that, in January 1993, there were 117 million people aged 50 years and over and nearly 75 million older people aged 60 and over in the 15 countries of the newly expanded EU. This represents nearly 32 per cent and 20 per cent respectively of the total population of the EU.

In 1993[1] nearly one-third of the Union's population and one-fifth of the labour force were over the age of 50. The data indicate that by the year 2000 people aged over 60 will comprise more than one-fifth of the population and, by 2020, they will represent more than one-quarter (see Figure 2.1). What is perhaps more significant in policy terms is the increase in the numbers of people over 80, the majority of whom are women. However, rather than viewing these trends with alarm, they should be viewed as a positive outcome of advanced socio-economic development.

Women predominate in the higher ranges of the 'age pyramid' for all the countries of Europe so that, as the population of each member state ages, it becomes increasingly 'feminized' (see Figure 2.2). For example, in the UK at the last census, in 1991, there were almost 10 million (9.951 million) women over 50, and of those over state pensionable age, women comprised 12 per cent of the UK population and men six per cent. In 1993 for the Union as a whole, among those aged 45–9, the numbers of men and women were roughly equal; at the ages 70–4 there were four women for every three men; at 80–4 there were two women for every man; and by the ages of 95 and over, the ratio was more than three to one.

There are quite wide variations in sex ratios between member states, particularly in the oldest group (95+). For example, in January 1994 the female/male ratio in France, Austria, Finland, Denmark, and the UK was equal to or greater than five to one; in Belgium and Sweden four to one; in Ireland, the Netherlands, and Spain three to one and in Greece it was nearly two to one.

Not unrelated to this are the increasing divorce rates in EU states. Even though many divorcing people will remarry, this has important policy implications for the future income of older women, particularly in terms of their pensions (see Chapter 4) and, more generally, their social integration. The 'crude divorce rate' for the EU as a whole has risen from 0.5 per 1000 of the population in 1960 to 1.7 per 1000 of the population today. The UK has the highest divorce rate among all the EU states at 3.1 per 1000 in 1993. Excluding Ireland, where divorce has only very recently been permitted under its constitution, the lowest is in another Catholic country, Italy. Also, there is a higher proportion of widows than widowers in the EU. Hence it should be clear to national and European policy makers and practitioners alike that a greater focus upon the social and economic position of older women must have a higher priority.

Not only is the EU an ageing community, but the transformation in the age structure of the population is taking place in a remarkably short time. As we

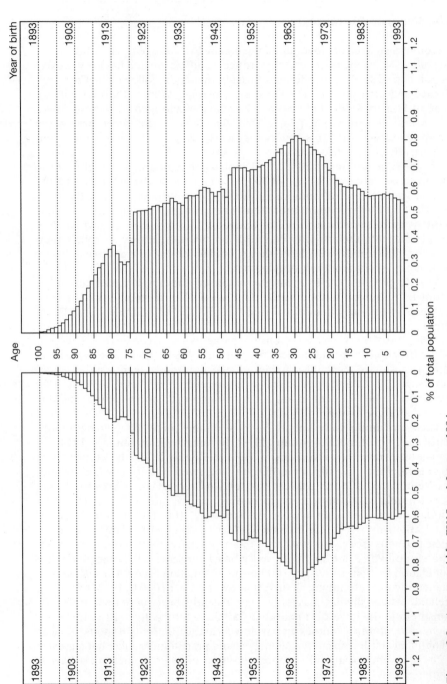

Figure 2.2 Age pyramid for EU15 on 1 January 1994.
Source: Eurostat, *Demographic Statistics*, 1995, B7, p. 28. Luxembourg: Eurostat.

noted above, although there are variations between the constituent states of the EU in the precise influence of each of the various factors contributing to this change (and some special factors such as the impact of migration in the case of Greece), the two main factors are declining fertility and mortality rates, as Tables 2.1 and 2.2 show. Table 2.2 shows that female life expectancy exceeds male life expectancy in all member states. For men, Sweden (closely followed by Greece) has the highest life expectancy at birth, 75.5 years, and Portugal the lowest, at 70.6 years. Life expectancy at birth for women is, on average, generally greater than for men, by approximately six years, with French and Spanish women (who live the longest) having a life expectancy at birth of around 80 years. Even Danish and Portuguese women (who have the lowest life expectancy among women in the EU) have a life expectancy at birth of 77.8 years. What should be noted about this table is that since 1960, life expectancy has increased for men by six years and for women by around seven years.

At age 60, life expectancy for men is between a low of 17.1 years in Ireland and high of 19.7 years in Greece. There are greater differences at age 60 for women, with life expectancy for French, Spanish and Swedish women being 24.6, 23.9 and 23.4 years respectively, and around 21 years in Denmark, Ireland and Portugal.

Not unrelated to these gendered differences in life expectancy is the increasing number of older people in Europe who live alone. This can also be regarded as a gendered phenomenon. According to the latest figures from Eurostat, 15 per cent of those aged 60–4 live alone. This percentage doubles for those 70–4 and is almost 48 per cent for those aged over 80. However, there are regional differences. For the northern states (i.e. the UK, Belgium, the Netherlands and France) more than half of those aged over 80 live alone, whereas fewer than 30 per cent live alone in Greece and Portugal and only 17 per cent do so in Spain. The reasons for these trends are complex and require further research. Hence, taking all this evidence into account, it should be clear to national and European policy makers and practitioners alike that a greater focus upon the social and economic position of older women must have a higher priority.

The changing nature of old age

Alongside the ageing of the population in Europe, we are witnessing a profound transformation in the experience and meaning of old age in late-twentieth-century society. Retirement is no longer the straightforward entry point to old age that it once was and, therefore, it is increasingly anachronistic as a definition of older people. More and more people through-out the EU are leaving the labour force in different ways: early retirement, partial retirement, redundancy, unemployment, disability, and so on. At the same time, with increased longevity, older people are living longer and healthier old ages and, as a result, the threshold of frailty is being pushed back. These changes in age structure, health and patterns of employment are transforming the nature of old age. They are, thereby, posing sharp questions about both the traditional, passive roles expected of older people and the extent to which policy makers and major economic and political institutions

Table 2.1 Total fertility rate for all 15 EU states, 1960–93

	EU15	B	DK	G	GR	SP	F	IRL	I	L	NL	A	P	FIN	SW	UK
1960	–	2.56	2.54	2.37	2.28	2.86	2.73	3.76	2.41	2.28	3.12	2.69	3.17	2.72	2.20	2.71
1970	–	2.25	1.95	2.03	2.39	2.90	2.47	3.93	2.42	1.98	2.57	2.29	3.02	1.83	1.92	2.45
1980	1.82	1.68	1.55	1.56	2.21	2.20	1.95	3.25	1.64	1.49	1.60	1.62	2.18	1.63	1.68	1.90
1990	1.56	1.62	1.67	1.45	1.39	1.34	1.78	2.12	1.30	1.61	1.62	1.46	1.57	1.78	2.13	1.83
1993	1.46*	1.59*	1.75	1.28	1.34	1.26	1.65p	1.93	1.22*	1.70	1.57	1.48	1.52	1.81	1.99	1.75

* = Estimates.

p = Provisional data.

Abbreviations (used in all subsequent tables): EU15, all 15 member states; B, Belgium; DK, Denmark; G, Germany; GR, Greece; SP, Spain; F, France; IRL, Ireland; I, Italy; L, Luxembourg; NL, Netherlands; A, Austria; P, Portugal; FIN, Finland; SW, Sweden.

Source: Eurostat, *Demographic statistics*, 1995.

Table 2.2 Expectation of life at birth, 1950–93

Men

	EU15	B	DK	G	GR	SP	F	IRL	I	L	NL	A	P	FIN	SW	UK
1950	–	62.0	69.8	64.6	63.4	59.8	62.9	64.5	63.7	63.4	70.6	–	56.4	–	71.2	66.2
1960	67.3*	67.7	70.4	66.9	67.3	67.4	66.9	68.1	67.2	66.5	71.5	66.2	61.2	65.5	72.2	67.9
1970	68.5*	67.8	70.7	67.4	70.1	69.2	68.4	68.8	69.0	67.1	70.7	66.5	64.2	66.5	72.8	68.7
1980	70.7*	70.0	71.2	70.2	72.2	72.5	70.2	70.2	70.6	69.1	75.7	69.0	67.7	69.2	74.8	70.2
1990	72.8	72.7	72.0	72.0	74.6	73.3	72.7	72.1	73.6	72.3	73.8	72.5	70.4	70.9	74.9	72.9
1993	73.0†	73.0	72.6	72.7	75.0	73.7†	73.3$_p$	72.7	–	72.2	74	72.9	70.6	72.1	75.5	73.6†

Women

	EU15	B	DK	G	GR	SP	F	IRL	I	L	NL	A	P	FIN	SW	UK
1950	–	67.3	–	68.5	66.7	64.3	68.5	67.2	67.2	68.2	72.9	–	61.6	–	–	–
1960	72.7*	73.5	74.4	72.4	72.4	72.2	73.6	71.9	72.3	72.2	75.3	72.7	66.8	72.5	74.9	73.7
1970	74.8*	74.2	75.9	73.8	73.8	74.8	75.9	73.5	74.9	73.4	76.5	73.4	70.8	75.0	77.1	75
1980	77.4*	76.8	77.3	76.9	76.8	78.6	78.4	75.6	77.4	75.9	79.3	76.1	75.2	77.6	78.8	76.2
1990	79.4	79.4	77.7	78.7	79.5	80.4	80.9	77.6	80.2	78.5	80.9	79.1	77.4	78.9	80.4	78.5
1993	–	79.9	77.8	79.2	79.9	81.0†	81.5$_p$	78.2	–	79.4	80.0	79.4	77.8	79.5	80.8	79.0†

Notes:
† = Data for 1992.
Data for Germany 1950–80 for FRG only.
* = EU12 figures.
$_p$ = Provisional figures.
– = No figure available.
Source: Eurostat.

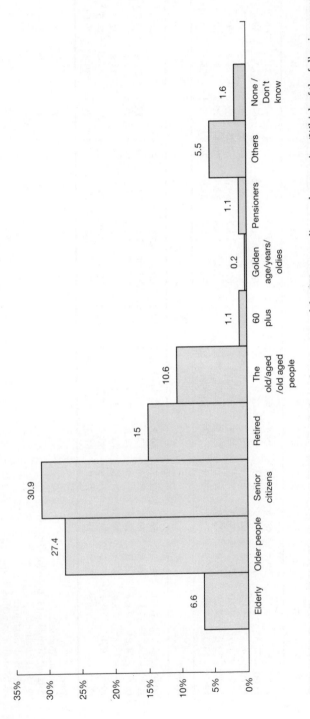

Figure 2.3 Choosing a name. Percentages of older people from the 12 states of the EU responding to the question 'Which of the following ways of describing people aged 60 and over is the one you prefer to be used?' (respondents could add their own terms).

have adjusted to sociodemographic change. In essence the question at issue is what is the place of older citizens in European society in the late twentieth and early twenty-first centuries?

In the light of the changing meaning of old age and the increasingly active stance being taken by senior citizens on a local, national and European level (Chapter 7), the terminology used to describe this group and the associated metaphors – elderly, old, retired – seem to be out of tune with their subjects. This is the reason why the distinction is now commonly made between the third age (50–74) – seen as the period of life when, freed from paid work and parenting, people can involve themselves in active, independent life – and the fourth age (75 and over) – the age of eventual dependence (Laslett 1987, 1994; Midwinter 1991). Indeed, the study sponsored by the Carnegie Institute (Carnegie Institute 1993) mentioned earlier used such a classification of old age.

However, it should be noted that even though this may be a more sensitive approach, emphasizing stages rather than age, it may not in practice reflect functional reality in many cases. Indeed, Ginn and Arber (1995: 8) have more recently suggested that Laslett's conceptualization of a 'third age' as a time for active leisure between retirement and increasing frailty 'is essentially a bourgeois option, unavailable to those who have low incomes and poor health', many of whom, as we shall see, also tend to be older women. Even though the opportunity may be present for older people, and in particular older women, to engage in different activities and adopt new identities, many in practice do not, since their primary role tends to be occupied around their continuing family and domestic obligations, so that they have less free time than older men (Bernard and Meade 1993).

What is in a name?

The Eurobarometer survey cut through much of the agonizing that has taken place, particularly in academic circles, about the appropriate nomenclature by asking older people themselves the direct question: what do *you* prefer to be called. The results are shown in Figure 2.3. As can be seen, there is no consensus across the whole of the 12 countries sampled, with the majority vote being split between 'senior citizens' and 'older people'. Four individual countries (Spain, Portugal, Luxembourg and Greece) showed a majority favouring 'older people' and three (Germany, Ireland and the UK) 'senior citizens'. What is abundantly clear though is that, with the exception of Denmark and the partial exception of the Netherlands, the term most commonly used by policy makers, the media and social gerontologists, that is, 'elderly', is firmly rejected.

In some countries there seems to be a reaction against connotations of 'oldness'. This was also one of the findings of the 1991 survey of attitudes to ageing in the UK (Midwinter 1991). The low proportion of UK senior citizens voting for 'older people', 'pensioners' and 'elderly' confirms that survey's findings. However, only Denmark and to a lesser extent Ireland and the Netherlands share this reaction and if they are excluded, along with the UK, 'older people' is strongly favoured. In contrast Italians seem to embrace the concept of oldness wholeheartedly, with two out of three people favouring 'older people' or 'the old'/'the aged'/'old aged people'.

The positive choice of 'senior citizens' over the whole of the 12 countries sampled is interesting and perhaps itself indicative of the changing character of old age in Europe. It carries connotations of individuals as civic actors with both rights and duties and, therefore, emphasizes the integration of older people rather than their separate group status. It had been thought, particularly by the author of the Eurobarometer questionnnaires, to be too closely associated with the USA to catch on here. But older people in Germany, Ireland and the UK backed it strongly, though in Germany it was the people of the western *Länder* that swung the vote.

The sweeping rejection of the media inspired 'golden age', with its soporific image of a 'golden pond' and obvious suggestions of comfortable affluence, is not surprising: after all, the survey's respondents are living the reality of old age and they know that it rarely fits the cosy celluloid images. But, more than that, when coupled with the preference for 'senior citizens', this seems to signal some kind of positive statement from this group that either they want to be regarded as people, who just happen to be older than some others, or as citizens like the rest of the community.

There is much food for thought here because labels carry symbolic meanings; they tell us, and particularly those they are applied to, a great deal about the social role and status of the labelled. If one can draw out a message from these results it is perhaps that those of us in the professional business of regularly putting a name to this large and growing group of EU citizens have not listened closely enough hitherto to what they want us to call them.

Respect for one's elders?

In the light of this, other questions may be raised. For example, are people treated with greater respect after they reach old age or is the opposite the case? The answer coming from the Eurobarometer survey, for the EU as a whole, is roughly balanced, with some three out of ten saying more and slightly fewer saying less. This leaves a majority responding (spontaneously) that they have detected no significant difference in attitude towards them. Interestingly there appears to be some association between age and the treatment older people feel they receive from others: 26 per cent of the 60–4-year-olds say that they have received more respect but this rises to 35 per cent among those aged 75 and over. The variations between countries are shown in Table 2.3.

In order to pinpoint more precisely whether or not older people have experienced patronizing, demeaning, derogatory or age-discriminatory atti-tudes from particular agencies, the survey asked them if they had ever been treated in this way by a wide range of different public and commercial agencies, professionals, the media and finally their own families. The most striking fact to emerge from this series of questions (apart from the exposure of the legal profession as paragons of virtue in this respect) is the small proportion of older people who have ever felt they have been treated as second-class citizens. This is encouraging news from our ageing societies. On the down side, though, concentrating on the minority that have been patronized or demeaned in some

Table 2.3 Proportion of older people saying they get
treated with more or less respect as they grow older

	More respect (%)	Less respect (%)
Belgium	19	33
Denmark	19	15
France	34	26
Germany	24	31
Greece	43	30
Ireland	44	21
Italy	33	26
Luxembourg	29	21
Netherlands	20	28
Portugal	34	13
Spain	33	28
UK	34	25

Table 2.4 Proportion saying they have been treated
as second-class citizens (EU12 as a whole)

Agencies/individuals	%
Social security/pensions	18
Local authorities	19
Banks/financial institutions	10
Doctors/health service	13
Post Office	10
Shopkeepers	13
Politicians	19
Transport staff	13
Media	16
Solicitors/lawyers	6
Their own family	8

way, it is public agencies and politicians that appear to be the worse culprits
(Table 2.4).

There were considerable variations between countries. For example, families came off worse in Belgium (17 per cent saying that they have been treated
as second-class citizens by their own families) and the legal profession in
Greece (13 per cent). The media was clearly worse than the average in
Germany (19 per cent and particularly in the old FRG, at 20 per cent); transport
staff in Portugal (21 per cent) and Greece (19 per cent); politicians in Germany
(26 per cent), Italy (24 per cent) and Belgium (23 per cent); shopkeepers in
Germany and Greece (21 per cent), while the UK (the 'nation of shopkeepers')
had a low score of nine per cent; post offices in Italy (18 per cent); doctors in
Greece (23 per cent) and Italy (19 per cent); banks in Greece (19 per cent) and
Belgium (16 per cent); local authorities in Germany (27 per cent), Greece and

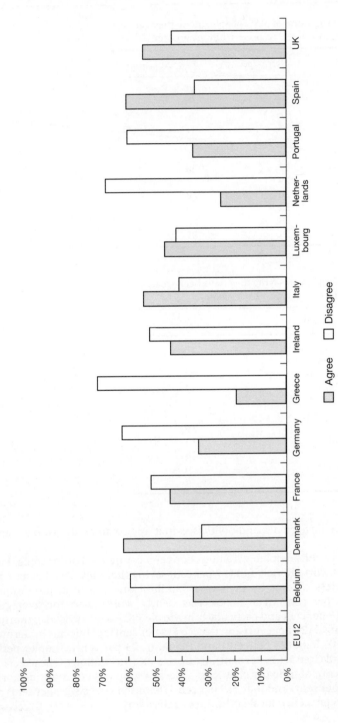

Figure 2.4 Responses to the proposition 'Old age has given me a new lease of life' (older people only).

Italy (24 per cent) and Belgium (23 per cent); and social security offices in Belgium, Greece and Portugal (25 per cent).

Of course, agencies and professionals named in this 'rogues' gallery' could reasonably protest that these results may tell us as much about the older people themselves as about the way they have been treated. There is something in that, but it cannot explain the whole picture. There were enough inconsistent variations between countries – with one exception – to suggest that the explanation lies beyond a predilection to criticize in a particular culture.

The exception, by the way, was Denmark, which consistently attracted the lowest score across ten of the 11 agencies and individuals. (The only one it did not score lowest on was 'politicians'; they appear to be at their least patronizing in the UK.) Perhaps Danish senior citizens are less prone to criticize than those of other countries, but this still does not explain the other variations across countries. And yet perhaps older citizens are actually treated differently in Denmark than in other EU countries. Maybe the bus drivers of Athens and Lisbon do have something to learn from their counterparts in Copenhagen, as do social security staff and families too. This issue certainly deserves further investigation and could give rise to a sharing of experiences across the EU that has the potential truly to fulfil the meaning of Union.

Older and better?

Two questions, 'How do older people respond to the ageing process?' and 'Has growing older given them a new lease of life?', are often posed by academics and the media. It was not until the Eurobarometer survey that a comparison was possible across all 12 European countries of the EU. There were some surprising results and these are presented in Figure 2.4. The obvious intention behind these questions was to dispense with the negative images of ageing and to put the positive case.

The mean score of the four responses falls roughly in the middle, as if the older citizens of Europe were equivocal about the experience. Perhaps, like the rest of life, it is a matter of good and bad points in their eyes. Looking at variations between countries, the difference between Denmark and Greece in the proportions agreeing strongly with the statement is no doubt partly attributable to the superior objective conditions of older Danes from their Greek counterparts, as we document in the forthcoming chapters. Explaining the even higher score for Spain requires further research in that country. In terms of differences based on age, for the sample as a whole, they are relatively small: overall, 52 per cent disagreed that growing older has given them a new lease of life compared with 41 per cent of those aged 75 and over. Not surprisingly, older disabled people were less likely to respond positively to this proposition: 39 per cent compared with 49 per cent for the non-disabled.

Passing the time

Many of the popular and literary images of old age are essentially passive images. For example, there are the sixth and seventh ages of Shakespeare's well known seven ages of man, and W. B. Yates says, 'When you are old and

Table 2.5 Passing the time (older people only) (percentages)

	EU12	B	D	F	G	GR	IRL	I	L	NL	P	SP	UK
There is hardly enough time in the day. I'm very busy	33.9	23.3	35.8	31.7	33.1	13.9	30.8	47.4	24.0	23.4	14.3	22.5	40.7
I have a full day but not too much to do	33.1	44.3	53.0	36.7	37.7	24.1	38.9	19.9	49.4	55.6	39.3	26.9	30.8
I have plenty of free time	23.5	21.9	7.9	20.9	21.6	39.6	20.4	23.3	18.0	15.3	31.0	38.6	21.5
I have so little to do. I often have too much time on my hands	6.0	5.3	2.0	7.5	5.1	11.9	6.4	5.2	5.6	4.8	9.2	8.7	4.3
I have nothing to do	2.9	4.7	0.9	3.2	1.5	9.1	3.0	3.4	2.4	0.7	6.2	4.2	2.2
Don't know	0.6	0.6	0.5	0.0	1.0	1.4	0.5	0.7	0.6	0.2	0.0	1.2	0.0

grey and full of sleep, and nodding by the fire . . .'. Indeed, US and British research on the image of older people portrayed in classical literature and poetry suggests that it is negative, focusing overly on the physical aspects of old age (Sohngen and Smith 1978; Till 1993) and again reflecting perhaps the persistence of ageism within Western societies. The reality is quite different. The picture to emerge from the Eurobarometer survey (see Table 2.5) is very much one of older people as active citizens. On average two out of three reported that they were either very busy or leading full lives.

The most active were the Italians, followed by the British; the least active were the Greeks and Portuguese. Eschewing any idea of convenient cultural stereotypes, it does appear that there was a void in the lives of a significant group of older people in both of these southern European countries. It is a sad fact that one in five in Greece and one in seven in Portugal said that they either have too much time on their hands or have nothing to do. The work of the Observatory on Ageing and Older People has demonstrated that policy makers are aware of this problem but there is clearly room for more actions to boost the social integration of older people, along the lines of the KAPI (community centres) in Greece.

Not surprisingly, there were variations between the third and fourth ages in answer to this question. For example, the proportion of those aged 60–64 leading busy lives was double that of those aged 75 and over (45 per cent versus 22 per cent), and while only one per cent of the former said they have nothing to do, six per cent of the latter said so. Those suffering from a longstanding illness or disability are only slightly less active than their non-disabled counterparts.

When we look at the kinds of activities older people are engaged in, this active picture is confirmed, even though the 'activity' undertaken by the largest number of them in the last week was watching television. Looking beyond that near universal pastime (at least nine out of ten people in all countries) there are routine daily tasks, such as shopping and housework, that seven out of ten of those questioned said they did last week. The UK came top of the shopping league (85 per cent) and Spain bottom (54 per cent). Danes appeared to do the most housework (81 per cent) and Spaniards the least (54 per cent).

Two out of five older people were engaged in gardening or do-it-yourself (DIY) household maintenance. Denmark and the UK are the countries where older people were most frequently involved in these tasks (three out of five) and Spain was where they have the lowest involvement (one in seven). Not surprisingly, it was primarily in the youngest age group (60–4) that gardening or DIY was most often mentioned. Over half of older people said that they went for a walk or took exercise in the previous week (three out of five in Denmark, Germany, Ireland, Spain and the UK), though less of those aged 75 and over (48 per cent) than the younger group (58 per cent). Nearly one in three older people had been to church or taken part in a religious meeting in the previous seven days. This rose to 82 per cent in Ireland, and dropped to 15 per cent in Denmark and 23 per cent in France and the UK.

Older people are less often engaged in extra-familial social pastimes: on average one in seven had been to a club or centre for senior citizens. The fact that the proportion using such centres in Denmark was three times that in Greece and Portugal (24 per cent compared with eight per cent) is bound to owe something to the very different levels of provision of these facilities between the north and south of the Union.

The use of social amenities intended not only for older people, including social clubs and bars, was nearly as common as for the special facilities (13 per cent on average). More than one-fifth of older people in Portugal and the UK had visited such a place in the previous week and this rose to a high of three out of ten in Ireland. The participation rate for cinemas, theatres and concerts was universally low (four per cent on average).

A small proportion of older people were engaged in organized voluntary work – eight per cent overall – but in Denmark, France, Ireland and the UK it rose to over ten per cent and in Luxembourg and the Netherlands it reached 17 per cent. However, in response to a specific question concerning membership of voluntary organizations and charities (as opposed to active engagement) more than one in eight responded positively. This proportion reached more than one in four in Denmark, Luxembourg and the Netherlands.

On the evidence of the Eurobarometer survey, European senior citizens are, by and large, involved in current affairs, with nearly three out of four having read a newspaper or magazine recently. In some countries this figure exceeded nine out of ten (Denmark, Ireland and the former GDR), but in Greece, Portugal and Spain it was much lower – around two in five. This points to the twin issues of access and ability: it is not simply that some older people in these southern states do not have the resources to purchase newspapers and magazines but also that levels of illiteracy are still higher than average among the older age group (Chapter 7). However, senior citizens in the EU cannot be described as 'bookworms' – only one in three had read a book in the previous week. In only two countries (the Netherlands and the UK) did this proportion exceed 50 per cent. Again Greece, Portugal and Spain returned the lowest figures (10–14 per cent).

This account started by pointing to the relatively high levels of activity revealed by the survey. When it came to political activity, however, the story was quite different. Only just over one in 100 older people had taken part in political or pressure group activities in the previous seven days. This increased to three in 100 in Italy and Luxembourg and four in 100 in the former GDR.

This does not mean that older Europeans are not *interested* in politics. We asked them about the issues that interest them and more than one in five said local politics and one in four national politics. More than two out of five said they are interested in major social problems such as human rights, poverty and homelessness, while nearly half are interested in the environment. These findings suggest a fair degree of latent political and social commitment among older people and certainly disprove any suggestion that they might have disengaged from civic life. We consider these issues at greater length in Chapter 7.

Intimacy at a distance

As was noted earlier in this chapter, the trend for increasing numbers of older people to live alone may be observed in all EU countries – though it is more

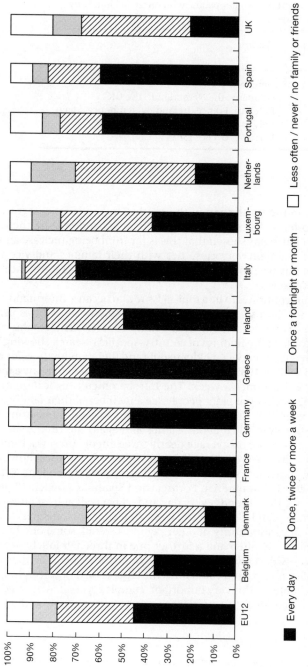

Figure 2.5 Contacts with family and friends (older people only).

- ■ Every day
- ▨ Once, twice or more a week
- ▧ Once a fortnight or month
- □ Less often / never / no family or friends

Table 2.6 Proportion of older people who often feel lonely by country (percentages)

Percentage feeling lonely often	Country
<5	Denmark
5–9	Germany, the Netherlands, the UK
10–14	Belgium, France, Ireland, Luxembourg, Spain
15–19	Italy
20 or more	Portugal, Greece (36%)

pronounced in the north than in the south. Thus residential segregation has given rise to fears that older people are being abandoned by their families. Research evidence has shown that this is far from being the case and, in fact, older people maintain very close ties with their families and vice versa – a position that has been perfectly described as 'intimacy at a distance' (Rosenmayer and Kockeis 1963).

Because this continues to be a topical issue and because information on some EU countries is hard to come by, the Eurobarometer survey was used to ask older people themselves about their family contacts. The results, shown in Figure 2.5, confirm the findings of country-specific research showing frequent face-to-face contacts between older people and their families (see, for example, Qureshi and Walker 1989). On average nearly four out of five saw a member of their family at least once a week. The Eurobarometer replication in Sweden found that 32 per cent of older people see a member of their family every day and 70 per cent at least once a week (Andersson and Sundström 1996). A similar question was asked about friends and again the results showed high levels of social contact: on average nearly three out of four saw a friend at least once a week. There were wide differences between countries, however, with less than one in ten seeing a friend every day in Germany and the Netherlands compared with six out of ten in Portugal and Spain. In Sweden 17 per cent of older people see their friends every day and 69 per cent at least once per week.

Despite these high levels of social contact, feelings of loneliness are present among a significant minority of older people. Overall, some one in eight said that they felt lonely often and a further one in three felt lonely occasionally. But there are wide variations between countries (Table 2.6) that might be noted by policy makers and could form the basis of further research. We return in the next chapter to this very important, complex, yet often over-generalized issue when we consider the social integration of older people in the EU.

Note

1 The following data refer to the 12 countries that comprised the EU at that time and therefore do not include Austria, Finland and Sweden. They are derived from the data obtained for the European Observatory.

3

Intergenerational relations and social integration

This chapter considers the social integration of older people and relations between generations in the EU states. These two issues were a central feature of the 1993 European Year and, arguably, are vital to the fabric of European society itself. There are many references to this sometimes vexed issue scattered throughout classic Western literature – Job and his sons, Oedipus, King Lear and his daughters – so we know that it is an age-old one. But what is the current state of relations between the generations? What do older people think of younger people? Do older people favour age segregation? And, crucially in policy terms, what is the future of the social contract between the generations? Will the generations in employment continue to pay for the pensions of those in retirement? Some answers to these questions come from the Eurobarometer survey as well as from the research of the European Observatory on Ageing and Older People.

Young versus old?

There is much conventional wisdom about the lack of respect for older people on the part of the young, so the older Europeans in the Eurobarometer survey were asked whether or not they agree with the statement that 'Young people are generally helpful towards older people'. The question was purposely positive to avoid the promotion of a popular negative stereotype. The results indicate that, on the whole, older people are favourably inclined towards the young, with an average 58 per cent of all the people aged 60 and over surveyed agreeing with the statement. Older people in Denmark and Ireland stand out as being the most positive about youth, with those in agreement representing 75 and nearly 82 per cent respectively. Those questioned in Belgium and Italy are the least positive, with 53 and 42 per cent respectively agreeing with the statement. Those in their fourth age were more likely to agree strongly with the

Table 3.1 Older people's contact with people younger than 25 (percentages)

	EU12	B	D	F	G	GR	IRL	I	L	NL	P	SP	UK
A lot	36.4	40.3	45.5	33.8	36.5	27.8	46.4	37.7	39.5	37.2	32.5	26.4	42.2
A little	35.6	33.2	31.8	30.1	39.0	36.7	30.1	38.8	24.8	32.2	44.4	37.9	32.2
Hardly any	18.6	16.1	14.5	20.9	18.0	16.8	17.4	15.2	21.6	23.3	17.1	24.1	18.3
None at all	9.1	10.0	7.7	15.2	6.0	18.3	6.1	8.4	14.1	7.2	6.1	11.3	7.3
Don't know	0.2	0.4	0.6	0.0	0.6	0.4	0.0	0.0	0.0	0.1	0.0	0.3	0.0

proposition that young people are helpful to older people than those in their third age.

An attempt was also made in constructing the questionnaire for the 1992 survey of older people to provide a comparison with the 1990 Eurobarometer study of young people's attitudes to the major issues of the day. This proved impossible and the Eurobarometer survey had to settle for a differently worded question, but we are able to draw a very loose comparison between some of the causes espoused by younger and older people.

On average nearly half of older people professed an interest in the environment (ranging from 69 per cent in Luxembourg to 30 per cent in Spain); in the 1990 survey 56 per cent of 15–24-year-olds saw this as one of their 'greatest causes'. Just over two out of five older people are interested in major social problems such as human rights and poverty (from 54 per cent in Greece to 26 per cent in Belgium), while just under two out of five younger people said that poverty was one of their greatest causes and nearly half said human rights. The proportion of young people interested in Third World issues is double that of older people (29 per cent compared with 14 per cent). World peace was the dominant cause in the 1990 survey of young people (60 per cent) but among older people only slightly more than one in ten expressed an interest in it (from 36 per cent in Greece to 4 per cent in Spain). Finally, the proportion of older people interested in religious life was more than four times that suggested for young people by the 1990 survey (32 per cent compared with seven per cent).

Intergenerational contact

In order to assess the current state of relations between the generations, it is essential to know how much contact there is between them as well as the nature of that contact. To this end the straightforward question was asked: 'How much contact do you have with young people, say younger than 25, including members of your family?' The results shown in Table 3.1 reveal a high level of interaction between young and old. Not surprisingly, the amount of contact declines with age: 46 per cent of those aged 60–4 report a lot of contact compared with 27 per cent of those aged 75 and over, while 6 per cent and 14 per cent say none at all.

The follow-up question was: 'Would you like to have more contact with young people?' The results suggest ambivalence, 45 per cent wanting more and 25 per cent not (with ten per cent don't knows). However, when these averages are broken down by country, a clearer picture emerges. Thus, more than three in five older people in Greece, Italy and Portugal said that they want more contact with young people, and similarly large proportions in Denmark, the Netherlands and the UK said they do not.

Some questions were designed to probe the issue of age segregation from the perspective of older people. We asked this group whether older people prefer to mix with people of their own age. A majority agreed that they do: 24 per cent strongly and 35 per cent slightly, while only 11 per cent disagree strongly. The strongest agreements were in Greece and Portugal (44 per cent) followed by Spain (36 per cent), Ireland and Luxembourg (31 per cent). The strongest disagreements were in Denmark (26 per cent), the UK (18 per cent) and the Netherlands (16 per cent).

The results from this section of the survey of older people suggest, tentatively at this stage, that the interaction between young and old is relatively high and, as far as older people are concerned, it is high enough in most countries. It seems that senior citizens think that their age group prefers to mix with people of its own age. Furthermore, there does appear to be a significant minority, in a majority of member states, who would support the development of age-related political parties (Chapter 7).

This issue was also pursued in the Eurobarometer survey of general public opinion in member states. Again, the positive case was put: 'Older people are admired and respected by young people', and the public were asked to agree or disagree. A majority disagreed 63 per cent (two-thirds slightly and one-third strongly). The main deviations from this opinion were in Ireland and Portugal, where more than one-fifth agreed strongly with the proposition and more than half agreed either slightly or strongly.

So, as far as the general public is concerned, in a majority of member states, young people do *not* admire and respect older people. The reasons cannot be probed here but it may be reasonably asked, why should they? Because older people are older? The young may reasonably expect more than that. But let them speak for themselves: when the responses are broken down by age, the youngest age group (15–24) was slightly more inclined to the affirmative than those aged 55 and over: 38 per cent agreed that older people are admired and respected by young people as opposed to 31 per cent of those aged 55 and over.

A majority (69 per cent: one-third agreeing strongly and two-thirds slightly) of European public opinion also holds that older people are too set in their ways and ideas. The highest levels of disagreement were found in Denmark and Ireland, where 17 per cent and 13 per cent respectively, disagreed strongly compared with an average for the EU of seven per cent. The proposition that 'older people are not willing to listen to younger people's views' produced a split vote, with the average for the EU as a whole falling almost exactly in the middle of the possible responses. The countries showing the strongest agreement were Portugal, Luxembourg and Spain, and those disagreeing most strongly were Denmark, Ireland and the Netherlands.

Finally, in the general population survey we asked whether 'older people and younger people should mix together more often socially'. The response was a unanimous yes, with nine out of ten such respondents being split evenly between strong and slight agreement. The only countries slightly to oppose this trend were Belgium and the UK, but it must be emphasized that, even in those countries, there were still large majorities in favour of intergenerational social mixing.

Relations between the generations

The current state of relations between the generations, between the old and young, is important because, at a micro-level, such relations between kin form the bedrock of all human societies and, at a macro-level, they form the basis of the social contract implicit in all welfare states (Walker 1996). In all member

states of the EU, worries have been voiced recently about the policy implications of population ageing and these usually focus on one particular concern:
the rising 'dependency ratio' between older people and those of working age.
The deficiencies of these crude demographic tools have been exposed elsewhere but, nonetheless, dependency ratios are of pressing concern to some
policy makers and independent commentators (World Bank 1994; Taverne
1995; Anson 1996). Some go further by pointing to the potential for conflict
between workers and pensioners if the 'burden' of financing pensions is not
lifted (Bengston and Achenbaum 1993; Johnson *et al.* 1989).

If an informed debate is to take place in Europe it is important to establish
what the populations of the member states think about the payment of
contributions and taxes to fund pensions, or, in other words, the social
contract, which is often regarded as the 'acid test' of intergenerational
solidarity. The standard Eurobarometer (administered for the general public
aged 15 and over) asked to what extent people agreed or disagreed with the
proposition that those in employment have a duty to ensure, through the
contributions or taxes they pay, that older people have a decent standard of
living.

In fact, on the basis of the data from the Eurobarometer surveys, we can
pronounce *both* sets of relations between the generations to be in good health.
At the micro-level there are frequent contacts between younger and older
people and a generally favourable perception of the former by the latter
(Walker 1993b: 13). At the macro-level, with regard to the funding of
pensions, the results of the question in the previous paragraph, shown in
Figure 3.1, demonstrate a remarkably high level of consensus and suggest that
the social contract is in good shape. If there is any slight cause for concern it lies
in the fact that there was a tendency among those aged 15–24 and 25–34 not to
be as strong in their agreement as older age groups. For example, 28 per cent of
15–24-year-olds agreed strongly with the social contract proposition, compared with 40 per cent and 41 per cent of 55–64-year-olds and those aged 65
and over respectively. However, these groups were more likely than the older
ones to agree slightly, so the overall consensus was maintained.

Such results indicating the absence of intergenerational conflicts in the
member states were also reflected by Observatory experts and should be
regarded as something European societies should take great pride in. However,
policy makers must beware of complacency. There is no doubt that the
potential for intergenerational cleavage lies in some of the policy options
currently being implemented or debated in different member states, yet these
consequences are rarely considered in public discourse. For example, the
development of more rigidly generationally segmented labour markets and the
encouragement of more individually based pension entitlements may increase
the social distance between the generations. It should be noted that the
Eurobarometer survey found that younger adults have doubts about the
extent to which the pensions contract will be honoured in the future (Chapter
4).

The greater reliance on the family or more often female kin for care may
exacerbate intergenerational conflicts within the family. Ill-judged political
rhetoric too may play its part in encouraging antagonism between the

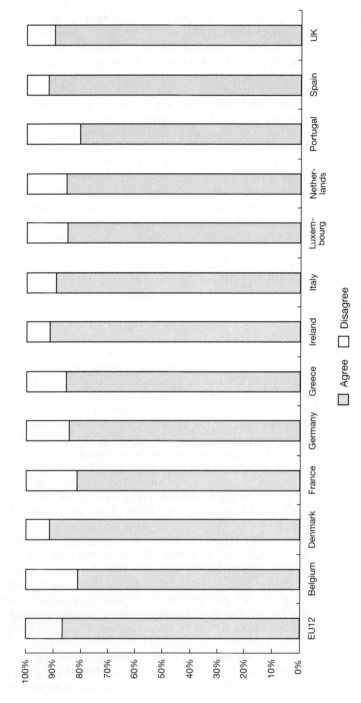

Figure 3.1 Results from preposition 'Those in employment have a duty to ensure, through contributions or taxes, that elderly people have a decent standard of living'.

generations, for example use of terms such as 'burden' with reference to old age. So, in facing up to the big questions concerning the funding of pensions and health care, policy makers must, at the very least, beware of unwittingly encouraging negative attitudes towards older people. A more positive direction was signposted in 1988 by the National Council for the Elderly in Ireland, which started an 'Age and Opportunity' programme in order to combat negative attitudes towards older people. In this respect, the 1993 European Year of Older People and Solidarity Between the Generations was of great importance precisely because it emphasized the issue of solidarity. Also, in very practical terms, the Commission established a European network of innovative projects concerned with the promotion of mutual assistance between generations and measures to foster the independence of older people. Thirty-six such projects formed the network, covering all 12 member states, and they reflected two main themes: care and housing schemes which stimulate both the autonomy and the integration of older people in society, and using the potentialities of older people. The network consists of successful examples of projects promoting solidarity between the generations (Flynn 1995). There are other examples of local action aimed at enhancing solidarity, such as the campaign in Portugal on intergenerational solidarity by the National Committee for Old Age Policy.

Social integration

As the period following labour force participation is extended, the need for new roles and new social meaning becomes a pressing one for older people. Yet the context in which this search for a new social meaning is taking place is a rapidly changing one. As was noted in the previous chapter, change is occurring not only in the sociodemographic structure, but also in the organization of production and consumption. Furthermore, in southern Europe, there is also rapid urbanization. Arguably, therefore, the maintenance of social integration is one of the central policy issues confronting all industrial societies, as well as a direct personal one being faced by millions of people, including senior citizens. Yet the major socio-economic changes taking place currently, for example in the labour market, are sometimes pulling in the direction of separation and *dis*-integration rather than integration.

More older people are surviving without families; those with families are entering new extended intergenerational caring relationships; economic insecurity in the labour market is increasing; and there is greater female participation in employment in most countries. These developments heighten the risks of isolation and alienation in advanced old age, or of conflict within the nuclear family over the provision of care. Thus a key challenge facing policy makers (and indeed senior citizens alike) in all EU countries is the maintenance and extension of social integration in conditions that may be hostile to that goal.

However, before continuing it may be instructive to outline what we mean when we refer to 'social integration' and why it is important. By the social integration of older people we mean, on the one hand, participation in social interactions, roles and relationships and, on the other, attachment to the commonly shared values and collective norms of the societies in which they live. In other words, integration consists of both exchange relationships and shared norms and values. As sociologists, such as Durkheim (1993, originally published 1893; 1952, originally published 1897), have recognized for more than a century, such integration forms an essential part of the social foundations of modern societies and it is part of the bonding that holds such societies together. Thus, the issue of social integration is, or should be, of major concern to policy makers.

Social integration is also concerned with participation, its opposite being social exclusion. Moreover, it is an active concept. Therefore, in order for older people to be socially integrated, societies must operate according to participative or active conceptions of old age, rather than the more familiar ones emphasizing dependence and senescence. This approach has been variously labelled by some social gerontologists 'participatory', 'active' or 'productive' ageing (Butler *et al.* 1990; Walker and Taylor 1993). It is underpinned by the notion that activity, or participation, in old age is healthy in both physical and mental terms. (The opposite is also true of course: health is an important determinant of participation.)

It is essential for policy makers to understand that social and economic policies may promote either exclusion or integration. Unless these two opposite potential outcomes are explicit in the policy-making process then negative consequences may happen by default. In other words, policy makers and practitioners need to be clear and open about the sort of images and experiences their policies are intended to create with regard to older people. Do they want to encourage the full participation of older people in the economic, social, political and cultural lives of their local, national and international communities, or marginalize them from mainstream society, so they end up banished from major sectors such as employment, and confined largely to private family relationships and artificial communities consisting only of older people themselves?

This is not to pretend that it is always easy to disentangle the various effects of social and economic policies with regard to integration and exclusion. A simple example is provided by the issue of whether or not older people should be granted concessionary prices for transport and entertainment. Most of us would agree that reduced prices for such services are an aid to integration in that they facilitate access for older people. However, if well intended concessions also confer a sort of second-class citizenship on older people and thus an inferior form of integration, they may reinforce attitudinal barriers to integration. This complex issue requires close investigation by social researchers. The active involvement of older people themselves should be the central focus of these investigations, so that policy makers can formulate policies which fully represent their feelings and experiences.

Such an approach was adopted in the Eurobarometer survey. Responses revealed a large percentage of the general public supporting price concessions for older people on gas, electricity, telephones and transport. Across the EU as a whole nearly three out of four people aged 15 and over supported such concessions. Yet older people themselves preferred raising pensions (49 per cent) to price concessions (35 per cent), with one in ten saying they wanted both. The largest difference in support for pensions versus concessions was found in Denmark (82 per cent versus 11 per cent), while the smallest was Belgium (45 per cent versus 36 per cent). Spain was the only country where a larger proportion of older people wanted reduced prices rather than higher pensions. These issues are discussed at greater length in the next chapter.

Living alone

There is a growing recognition that, as the population ages, an increasing proportion of older people are living alone. It should be recognized that this phenomenon is also gendered. Fears have been expressed in policy circles in every member state about the social isolation that may result from this growth of older people living alone. However, as the studies conducted by national experts for the European Observatory on Ageing and Older People have indicated, the majority of older people have children living with them, near them or who are in regular contact with them (Walker 1993a).

Three points should be stressed here. Largely as a result of greater longevity, those living alone in old age are more likely to be women than men, as the age pyramid (Figure 2.2) and the discussion in Chapter 2 demonstrated. Secondly, the trend towards separate dwellings is less pro-nounced in southern states than it is in the northern ones. In Greece, for example, where it is more common for lone households to occur in rural than urban settings, the latest figures (1982) indicate that only 4.7 per cent of people aged 65 and over were living alone. In Portugal similar figures for 1981 indicate that there were 17 per cent living alone. In contrast, in France, 16 per cent of older men and 40 per cent of older women live alone, and these proportions increase with age, so that among those aged 75 and over 20 per cent of men and 45 per cent of women live alone. In the UK a similar profile is noted, with 31 per cent of men and 58 per cent of women aged over 75 living alone. However, it should be stressed that living alone does not necessarily imply loneliness or social isolation. Finally, this trend towards separate dwellings has important policy implications. Not only are there implications for the provision of health and social services, particularly in home care, but also there is an association between living alone and poverty. Because those living alone are more likely to be women and especially divorced and separated women (for the reasons outlined in Chapter 4) they are particularly prone to poverty. This means that this group is at greater risk of multiple deprivation, where low incomes and poverty are compounded by poor or inadequate housing.

Some member states have taken some actions to counteract social isolation resulting from these trends. For example, in Portugal the 'familiar welcome' scheme was introduced in 1991. This runs along similar lines to family placement schemes found in parts of the UK and the 'boarding out' scheme introduced in Ireland in 1990, where families are paid to foster older people for short periods. In Greece, since 1979, there has been a growth of 'Open Care Centres for the Elderly', or KAPI, which help to combat isolation and aim to enhance wellbeing. There are over 257 such centres and the research evidence suggests that they have been successful in preventing isolation, increasing companionship and satisfying recreational needs.

Social integration of older people

The social integration of older people was investigated by the Observatory according to three main dimensions: informal/family and friendship networks; quasi-formal, volunteering activity; and formal economic and political institutions. The extent of conflict or cleavage between the generations in the member states (an issue that was given great prominence in the US in the 1980s) was also considered (Walker 1993b). We focus on some of the key findings contained in the studies conducted by experts from 12 EU states and then consider the remaining barriers to the integration of senior citizens in the EU today.

A striking feature of the expert reports is the contrast, in all member states, between the continuing close integration of the majority of senior citizens in the primary relationships of family and neighbourhood, and their exclusion from some of the key formal economic institutions, notably the labour market. As we consider each of these dimensions of social integration (the informal dimension in this chapter and the formal one in subsequent chapters) it is important to keep in mind the uneven distribution of integration and exclusion among older people even though, in most EU countries, it is a minority that suffers gross forms of exclusion.

Participation in informal relationships

Despite all that has been written about the break-up of the modern family, Observatory experts reported that, in all countries, older people remain integrated within their families (when they have them). Of course, much of the pessimism concerning the family stemmed from the growth of separate dwellings and the development of the modified extended family, with children living away from their parents: the notion of 'intimacy at a distance' referred to in the previous chapter.

We have highlighted previously the Eurobarometer finding that, on average, nearly four out of five older people in the EU see a member of their family or friends at least once a week (Figure 2.5). The reports from the Observatorys country experts corroborate this by showing the continuing high levels of family-based care, especially by spouses and daughters. Some reports also referred to the reciprocal flow of care from older to younger generations, such as the role of grandparents in the care of grandchildren in many of the countries studied. For example, Kuty's (1993) study on Belgium, documented how in Flanders one-quarter of children are looked after by their grandparents. Indeed, he noted that of the 53.3 per cent of all children regularly watched over by people other than their parents, 43.8 per cent 'are looked after by their grandparents'. This figure has remained at this level since 1983 despite the increased inclusion of women into the paid workforce in Flanders.

Observatory experts reported comparatively high levels of integration within family and neighbourhood life in all EU countries. However, such a conclusion must be qualified in five respects. First, particularly in the southern EU states, there are clear differences between rural and urban areas. For example, family solidarity may remain intact in rural areas but be threatened by industrialization and urbanization and, therefore, special policy measures will be required to ameliorate the impact of these processes on older people. Secondly, the tendency for an increasing proportion of older people to live alone – common to all EU countries – is, in part at least, a function of the combination of increased longevity and smaller families. This means that a growing number of older people will be surviving alone without family contacts and therefore will be at risk of social isolation. All Observatory country reports highlighted this issue and it is one that particularly affects women. Thirdly, intergenerational integration within the family will come under increasing pressure as a result of sociodemographic changes that are extending both the duration and the intensity of caring relationships in an unprecedented way. In this context it is vital that policy makers do not continue to take family care for granted and, by so doing, allow it to become overburdened (Qureshi and Walker 1989). Fourthly, the family in many countries is being subjected to considerable economic pressure, for example from unemployment, which is likely to limit its caring capacity. Finally, despite quite high levels of contact between older people and their families, feelings of loneliness are present in significant minorities of older people.

However, as we previously suggested, there may be a tendency on the part of some commentators towards over-generalization with regard to this complex issue. It is assumed in the gerontological literature that social interaction, especially with family members, is important to the wellbeing of older people and their adjustment to old age. Loneliness may be distinguished from living alone and social isolation. People may *feel* lonely despite frequent social contact (Tunstall 1966), perhaps owing to the loss of a spouse. Loneliness may be confined to particular parts of the day or, commonly in old age, to the night. Therefore, frequency of social contact may be taken as an indicator of the degree of social isolation. Another, more subjective and less frequently used indicator of loneliness is to ask older people if they feel lonely and if so, how often.

Evidence from the research conducted by the Observatorys experts indicates that the main difficulties appear to be confined to the southern states (see Table 2.6 and Walker 1993b). The northern ones display high levels of contact and satisfaction with contact on the part of older people; for example, in the Netherlands some 88 per cent are satisfied. With regard to the southern states the data are sometimes contradictory. A recent study in Italy found 50 per cent of those aged 65 and over feel lonely sometimes, yet 70 per cent of them see their relatives at least once per week (Florea *et al.* 1992). Clearly in this case, social contact and loneliness co-exist. There seems to be a suggestion here that older people in the southern states have a yearning for more frequent contact, perhaps a reflection of an idealized version of the family of their youth. Other evidence from Italy shows that older people living alone who are satisfied with their relationships with their children (i.e. see enough of them) are those who have other social relationships, such as friends and neighbours. In other words, loneliness is less of a burden when living alone is a personal choice and is accompanied by social relationships outside the family.

This finding is of the utmost importance in policy terms because it suggests that policy makers should not rely solely on the family (however constructed) as a source of social support. Also, the policy of community care, or the promotion of independent living, must include practical measures to encourage social support beyond the family. There are signs that policy makers in several countries have begun to tackle this issue. Examples include the Open Care Centres in Greece; the encouragement of volunteering in the Netherlands; in Germany the creation of contact and information centres in Berlin and Hamburg and projects such as 'self-reliance' in Munich; in Denmark the activity houses that are provided free of charge by municipalities for older people to meet and operate as they see fit (40 per cent of municipalities have such provision); in Portugal the 'familiar welcome' scheme (the provision of temporary or permanent integration within another family); in the UK the paid neighbours/helpers in some areas and in most areas, day centres; and in Italy recreation facilities provided for older people in some communes. So there is an array of different attempts to facilitate alternative sources of support and social integration within informal relations. None of them yet approaches universal availability, but there are plenty of good examples to build on and the Union itself is playing a leading role in disseminating examples of good practice (see for example Croft 1993). The vital role of 'volunteering', within a social policy on ageing, in the enhancement of social integration is considered in Chapter 7.

Participation in voluntary organizations

The ageing of the European population, the increasing activity of the third age, together with the increasing shift towards market-based solutions in welfare, as part of the encouragement of more pluralistic systems of provision, has focused attention upon voluntary action and voluntary activity in general in the EU. The EU as a political body has produced a white paper, *Association and Foundations*, and a number of organizations have compiled reports on the role of volunteering. The United Nations World Summit on Social Development, held in Copenhagen in March 1995, also made special reference to the importance of voluntary action within its final declaration. The aim of all these developments is the enhancement of voluntary activity, the creation of a newly formulated civil society and the movement towards a new civic Europe (Gaskin and Davis Smith 1995).

The European Observatory on Ageing and Older People also considered the role of voluntary action within the EU. The main concern was not so much with services or organizations provided for older people but their involvement in such service provision. More often the two are closely interrelated. At the time, and looking at 12 countries of the EU, older people had relatively low yet often vital involvement in voluntary activities. Although there are a (minority) of older people actively engaged in voluntary activity, more often such activity within EU countries is confined to those younger than 50 who provide services or assistance to older people. However, several countries, for example Ireland, Portugal and the UK, have seen the growth of professional senior consultants organizations. An example of this sort of development comes from Ireland, where the Irish Industrial Development Authority has introduced a scheme, called 'Mentor: A Helping Hand for Small Business', under which retired experts are contracted to companies as advisers on a short-term basis.

High rates of attendance of older people at clubs and organizations are seen in several countries. This has become particularly important over recent years. Such clubs and associations can actively enhance the social integration of older people into their societies. For example, in Germany, where 45 per cent of the population over 60 are members of such clubs, the Deutscher Turnerbund (German gymnastic association) started a campaign for 'sports for the elderly', which had the effect of introducing special initiatives for older people. Similarly in Denmark, there are approximately 200,000 people who are volunteers mainly in sports clubs (Hastrup 1995). These not only provide a social purpose but also act at the local level as pressure groups.

Ireland has seen a recent expansion in voluntary organizations providing services to older people: more than three-quarters of such organizations were established in the last 15 years. However, many of these are aimed at providing services for the very old. This is linked to the active encouragement and assistance by health boards and local authorities for voluntary bodies to become more involved in the provision of services for older people. This aside, high levels of voluntary activity among older people are also reported for Ireland: two-fifths of those aged 66–70 and one-fifth of 71–80-year-olds. Indeed, in terms of hours engaged in voluntary activity, older people compare very favourably with younger volunteers.

Italy has also seen a rapid increase in volunteering in terms of self-help groups and in organizations that assist a wide variety of 'at risk' groups. There has also been seen the need to set up a federal network of voluntary organizations to coordinate such activity. There are new self-help groups in Germany, which have experienced a substantial growth since the 1970s. It is thought that this is linked to the curtailment of public welfare and the growth of a more pluralistic or mixed economy of welfare. One study reported by the German expert showed that 27 per cent of all voluntary helpers are over 60 and roughly two-thirds are women (Alber 1993). He also reported that the main motivation for such involvement is for social contact with others.

In the Netherlands some 35 per cent of older people reported giving help to others. Also in the Netherlands a huge number of voluntary initiatives have been started recently, particularly by the early retired, some of which have an intergenerational support element, for example care services (meals provision, telephone circles and neighbourhood buses); communal living arrangements; education (study circles and discussion groups); and pressure-group activities. There is the 'Craft' project in Amsterdam, which has been running for nearly 12 years, in which older people use their knowledge and skills to teach younger people. It has spread, so that over 40 different communities have started similar projects. Some of these are run by older people themselves, and it is estimated that 4000 people have made use of these projects in the Amsterdam region alone.

In Spain voluntary organizations and other NGOs have a short history as a result of the long period under the Franco dictatorship, when such forms of social participation and activity were not possible. Perhaps because of this history the participation rates among older people are very low (e.g. around two per cent of the total number of Red Cross volunteers). Women volunteers predominate among older volunteers (54 per cent of the total) and nearly half of these are between 60 to 65 years of age. Spain's volunteer community is organized under an umbrella organization (La Plataforma par la Promoción del Voluntariados) that comprises 24 voluntary organizations (e.g. Caritas, Red Cross and Federation of Andaluzian Organisation of Older Persons (FOAM)) (*Ageing International* 1995b).

Unlike Spain, there is a long tradition of activity with voluntary organizations and involvement in voluntary work in the UK, especially with regard to the provision of assistance to older people. Some voluntary organizations, such as the Women's Royal Voluntary Service (WRVS), have for many years worked alongside the formal health and social services agencies to provide services such as meals-on-wheels. Though volunteers are not paid, organizations such as the WRVS are highly organized and provide services on a contractual basis.

According to the British General Household Survey (1987), involvement in voluntary work is concentrated among those in the 35–44 age group. Overall, more women (58 per cent) than men are involved in such work and 22 per cent, 13 per cent and seven per cent in the 45–59, 60–9 and over-70 age groups are involved in some form of voluntary activity. London and the south-east of England have the highest and the north of England the lowest proportions of voluntary activity. When acting as volunteers, older people involve themselves in activities which offer practical help to people or are involved in visiting people in institutions such as prisons, hospitals and residential accommodation for older people.

A more recent survey of involvement in voluntary action by older people formed part of the group of studies undertaken in the Carnegie Inquiry mentioned earlier (Carnegie Institute 1993). The study, which was conducted by Justin Davis-Smith from the Volunteer Centre in the UK, relied extensively upon data from the 1991 National Voluntary Activity (NVA) survey, which utilized a broad definition of voluntary activity and therefore demonstrated higher levels of activity than previous studies. However, the NVA study showed that 42 per cent of third agers had volunteered in the previous year as compared with 58 per cent of those aged 18–34 and 25 per cent of those over 75. It confirmed the findings of the previous General Household Survey studies, that women are more likely to volunteer than men and that older volunteers remain as volunteers for longer periods.

Turning to informal volunteering (i.e. visiting a sick person or relative, offering to undertake household chores or shopping for a neighbour or friend), there is still a high level of voluntary action, or perhaps more accurately, volunteering by older people. What the NVA does indicate, however, is that the frequency and the time spent in such activity gets less as age increases. This indicates a good level of both willingness to volunteer and social integration on the part of older people and perhaps also reflects increasing frailty.

We return to Gaskin and Davis Smith's study (1995), since this is one of the more recent surveys conducted which allows an evaluation of the extent of volunteering in Europe. The study focused upon ten European countries:

French-speaking Belgium, Bulgaria, Denmark, France, Germany, Great Britain, the Netherlands, Ireland, Slovakia, and Sweden. We shall focus only upon those countries which are members of the EU. The data were gathered by interviewing a representative sample of the resident population of each country. It should be noted that a very broad definition of the term 'volunteering' was used (although not employed in any of the questions) and a description of voluntary activity was read out to the respondent.[1] This issue of definition is a particular difficulty in collecting any comparative data in this area, since 'volunteering' can mean different things to different people and involve a variety of organizations and activities.

The survey found that just over a quarter of the population sampled had undertaken some form of voluntary activity. Belgium, the Netherlands, Sweden and Great Britain had the highest levels of volunteering, with the Netherlands demonstrating over 40 per cent of respondents indicating they had volunteered. The survey also confirms the Observatory's indications that volunteering is not widespread among older people and tends to decline after the age of 65. It is highest among those aged 35–54, although some countries (e.g. the Netherlands and Sweden) have similar levels of participation above 55 years. Most volunteering is undertaken for non-profit voluntary organizations and, aggregated across the EU countries, three-quarters of volunteers work for the voluntary sector. This figure is much higher for the Scandinavian countries (Sweden and Denmark) where respectively 89 per cent and 84 per cent work within the voluntary sector.

The most active area of voluntary activity is within sports and recreation, followed by social welfare or service-type activity, and then by education. Perhaps surprisingly, nearly a third of people over 65 who volunteered were active in social welfare provision. The main incentive for voluntary activity appears to come from the view that it is 'a moral and socially responsible activity that contributes to democratic society' (Gaskin and Davis Smith 1995: 62). However, most volunteers also report that it provides them with an opportunity for social interaction with people of a wide variety of ages and backgrounds, as well as more altruistic reasons.

Transport and communication

Transport and communication are also vital for the social integration of older people, a point noted by all the Observatory experts. For example, in the UK the British Gas survey (Midwinter 1991) found that the telephone is a valuable source of contact for 90 per cent of those living alone and an important means of communicating with grandchildren. Most countries have a system of travel concessions for older people; indeed, in Ireland free public transport is a universal entitlement for all older people. However, the variation in access to telephones is wide. For example, in western Germany, some 92 per cent of older people's households have telephones, and a similar proportion in the Netherlands have a telephone and/or an alarm. In Denmark the proportion is 97 per cent and in the UK more than 80 per cent of older people own a telephone, though there are significant variations with income. However, in Portugal, three-quarters of the most vulnerable older people (those aged 80 and over) lack a telephone. In Ireland the provision of free telephone rental for older people has increased the numbers of older people who have access to a telephone.

Summary

The findings of European research on older people show relatively high levels of integration within the informal relations of family and neighbourhood; indeed, many older people are active participants, providing services such as care. Certainly there are no indications of widespread isolation or anomie among Europe's older people. Suicide rates may be used as an indicator of anomie. Durkheim (1952) argued that 'suicide varies inversely with the degree of integration of the social group of which the individual forms part'. While suicide rates are higher among older than younger people and higher among older men than women, they have declined over time and remain relatively low. Nonetheless, the higher rates among older men than women (especially those aged 65–74) suggest the existence of role dissonance, even though older women are more likely to suffer acute deprivation (Chapter 4).

In contrast to the general picture of integration in primary or informal relations, the research reported in the next five chapters, especially Chapter 5, shows that older people have experienced increasing social exclusion from the major secondary, economic and political institutions in Europe.

Note

1 This description was as follows: 'The following questions are about time given freely and without pay to any organization which has the aim of benefiting people or a particular cause. This may involve any kind of activity or work which benefits the community, a group of people or an individual outside your family, although you may also in the process receive personal benefit for yourself or your immediate family. Unpaid work or activities done for the benefit of a cause such as the environment or animals is included.'

4

Pensions and living standards

For many years old age has been associated with poverty and low incomes, although there are signs that this situation is changing for the better in some EU countries. Although wide variation in living standards among older people in the various parts of the EU can be noted, the problems they face display various similarities and convergent trends. There are also divergences, particularly in the scale of the problems, in the pensions systems themselves, in the priority given to older people by policy makers and in the amount of success in tackling their problems.

Whatever the current trends, financial security is the bedrock of older people's social integration in EU countries as well as elsewhere. The importance of financial security in achieving European citizenship on the part of older people has been recognized by the EU in its Charter of the Fundamental Rights of Workers. This was adopted at the Strasbourg European Council on 9 December 1989, by all member states except for the UK, reaffirmed in the Council recommendation, of 27 July 1992, on the convergence of social protection objectives and policies (92/442/EEC), and formed part of the Social Chapter of the Maastricht Treaty. Particular mention should be made of paragraphs 24 and 25, which directly relate to the levels of old age pensions (24) and the minimum levels of social assistance (25) available in each member country:

24. Every worker of the European Community must, at the time of retirement, be able to enjoy resources affording him or her a decent standard of living.
25. Every person who has reached retirement age but who is not entitled to a pension or who does not have other means of subsistence must be entitled to sufficient resources and to medical and social assistance specifically suited to his (*sic*) needs.

This chapter therefore considers the incomes and living standards of older people in EU countries and highlights the results and the issues around financial security emanating from the Eurobarometer survey.

Gender inequalities

In all industrial societies, retirement income is built on four pillars: a basic pension provided by the state together with other social security income; a supplementary occupational pension; personal savings; and employment income (Reday-Mulvay 1990). It is a combination of the rights of access to these different sources of income and, more obviously, the level at which they are provided, that determines the economic and financial security of older people. Thus, and as other commentators have noted, financial and economic security in old age are primarily a function of the interaction of the socio-economic status individuals occupy during their working lives and the pension system that has developed in a particular country. Because of this relationship there are significant gender differences when considering the standards of living and incomes of older people, with women often having considerably lower living standards and levels of income in their old age than men (see Walker 1980, 1992; Arber and Ginn 1991; Groves 1992; Maltby 1994; Dooghe and Appleton 1995).

In Italy, for example, the median sum of old age pensions of women is 67 per cent of the male median; this difference is particularly noticeable for those aged 80 and over, where 34 per cent of female-headed households have incomes which are at the poverty threshold of 50 per cent of the average household income. However, recently proposals have been made to reform the structure of Italy's pension system. It is proposed to change from a defined benefit to a defined contributory system from 2013; the minimum retirement age will (initially) be set at 52 and rise to 57 by the year 2008. Although such reforms are subject to agreement between government and trade unions, it is hoped to have the effects of harmonizing the public-sector and private-sector pension systems; link benefits to contributions; establish a minimum retirement age; and create incentives for people to supplement private pension plans. If implemented, these proposals are likely to worsen the position of older women in retirement since the pension system will be even more closely aligned with the labour market.

In Germany the average pension paid to women in 1990 was just 42 per cent of the male average and, in 1989, women formed 76 per cent of the social-assistance recipients aged 60 and over, and a massive 83 per cent of those aged 75 and over.

Thus women, in particular widows, comprise some of the poorest and most socially excluded groups in the EU. However, Denmark is an exception, though even in that country there is a tendency among single people for men over 80 to have higher incomes than women in the same age group. Urgent action is required by policy makers to address this inferior socio-economic status of many older women in the EU. In particular, pensions policies in both public and private sectors must become more 'women friendly'.

Pension systems in the EU

Although financial security or insecurity in retirement is founded on four pillars, they are not of equal size and importance: throughout Europe it is the public pension system that is the main source of income for older people. This places the state in a special relationship with older people and emphasizes the vital importance of public policy in determining the living standards of this group of people. It also leaves them vulnerable to changes in entitlements to or levels of public pensions and, indeed, other social security benefits. Despite their different ideological, historical, political, administrative and cultural antecedents, it is possible to identify common elements in pension systems in the EU countries.

In most countries of the EU there are two tiers of pensions: the basic statutory pension schemes and the supplementary or complementary ones. Yet it should be remembered that there is considerable variation *within* them in the qualifying conditions for receipt of a pension and in the formulae used to calculate the earnings-related pension. However, the dominant pension model couples an earnings-related basic pension with a voluntary occupational one. It is important to note that such occupational pensions tend to favour male working patterns and lead to lower incomes for most women in their old age (Arber and Ginn 1991). There is also an increasingly important policy dilemma, particularly for the UK, over the issue of pension rights for women upon divorce. The recent publication of a green paper by the UK government on pensions splitting on divorce indicates its concerns (Department of Social Security 1996). Thus pension systems can maintain, often reflect and even enlarge socially structured gender inequalities created in the labour market and over the life course. These inequalities are also associated with the hierarchically structured power imbalances between men and women (Bury 1995; Ginn and Arber 1995).

The main exceptions in the EU are the Scandinavian countries – Denmark, Finland and Sweden – which all have a universal flat rate pension that is paid as a right of citizenship (according to residence) regardless of employment record, and a relatively undeveloped private occupational pension sector. This fact has major policy implications. The Danish pension system, like its Scandinavian counterparts, seems to have no inequalities based upon age or gender built into it, regardless of how they might arise in the labour market and over the life course. Moreover, there is a deliberate policy of redistribution, with the result that income distribution in old age is considerably flatter than among the employed. However, approximately one-third of all pensioners in Denmark have supplementary pensions. The spread of these pensions is likely to increase because of an agreement in 1991 between trade unions and employers to adopt them for the majority of the employed. This policy may also herald increasing age-cohort and related gender inequalities in Denmark.

In Finland, entitlement to the universal pension is granted for all Finnish citizens who have been resident for three years and to non-Finnish citizens who have been resident in Finland for five or more years immediately before receipt of the pension. The level of payment received relates to the length of residence, with a full amount paid to those resident for 40 years or more. Additionally, the earnings-related pension, which, like the universal pension, is funded through employment insurance, is based upon a statutory minimum and is calculated upon the best two years of earnings in the last four multiplied by the number of years of coverage up to maximum of 40 years.

The current Swedish pension system is undergoing radical reform. At present Sweden has a two-tier national system: a basic pension and a supplementary pension scheme. Entitlement to the universal basic pension is granted for those who have lived in Sweden for 40 years or worked there for 30 years. It is financed out of general revenue and contributions. Anyone who has worked in Sweden for 30 years is also entitled to the supplementary pension, which is calculated on the basis of the average of the best 15 years' income. In June 1995, the government outlined the major features of the new system, which were presented in a government bill in autumn 1995. It is intended to introduce the new system with a long transitional period commencing in 1997 and for it to be a compulsory national scheme. It will have an earnings-related part and will also ensure a guaranteed level of income for all those who have not earned any entitlement to a pension. Pensions will be based upon lifetime earnings, which include both earned income and social benefit income, which will also attract pension contributions. Child care, national service and educational studies after a certain age will also count towards pension rights. A flexible retirement age will be set from 61 years. The safety-net guaranteed pension will be set approximately at 38 per cent of the average full-time wage (for more detail see International Social Security Association 1995; Scherman 1995).

Outside Scandinavia, it is difficult to envisage how the notable gender imbalances in pension provision and income in old age can be equalized until economic parity is achieved between men and women, particularly in the labour market, and adequate compensation made for the effects of motherhood and other caring activities. Some non-Scandinavian countries have adopted a proactive stance towards enhancing the position of women in their national pension schemes. In Germany, for example, time spent outside paid employment providing care attracts increased pension credits. Yet such policies tend to focus on future pensioners. In the current ideological climate governments in various European countries tend to equate pension reform with cost containment and increasing the role of the private sector rather than addressing longstanding distributional issues.

Trends in living standards

The European Observatory on Ageing and Older People indicated that there are four main trends in the living standards and pension policies of EU countries. (The fourth is discussed under its own heading.) First of all, for the majority of countries studied, the living standards of older people have been rising in recent years. This progressive development is seen to derive from different factors in different countries and to be uneven in its impact on the older population. Therefore it is not possible to state unequivocally that the various social and economic policies of all member states have specifically targeted older people for improvement in living standards or that such policies have been universally beneficial.

Despite this caveat, in some cases the rising living standards of older people are the direct result of positive action by governments. For example, the French government has sought to raise the incomes of older people by extensions to the social assistance system and by indexing retirement pensions to net wages or prices, whichever is higher, so that they are tied to the rises in general living standards. As a result there has been a steep decline in the number of recipients of the minimum pension (*minimum viellesse*) over the last 30 years. Additionally, in Italy over the past 40 years the growth in the living standards of the older population is higher than that of the general population. In Luxembourg the National Programme for Older People was instituted in the early 1990s and from 1 January 1992 there was a ten per cent revaluation of contributory pensions and the introduction of a guaranteed minimum income aimed at combating poverty. The Spanish government has also actively sought to raise the living standards of older people by increasing the levels of minimum pensions. Some countries (e.g. Belgium, Greece, Italy and Luxembourg) have seen rises, albeit slight, in the numbers of older people receiving minimum social assistance benefits despite the rising standards of the population in general. However, it is a minority of governments that have adopted such proactive policies. In the majority of cases rising living standards appear to be a more passive by-product of improvements in the scope and coverage of occupational public pensions and the maturation of pension schemes introduced in the early post-war period (Organization for Economic Cooperation and Development (OECD) 1988).

The only member state to contradict this general rise of living standards is Portugal. Although there has been a rise in living standards since 1974 (the year of the revolution), the purchasing power of the old-age pension is declining. Thus, between 1988 and 1990 pension levels have decreased in comparison with corresponding levels of the minimum national wage and the whole population's standard of living. Additionally, in at least one country, Greece, there are major structural inequalities between pensions schemes applying in rural and urban areas. The main urban-based scheme (IKA) pays on average five times more than the average rural (OGA) pension. Added to this, within urban areas there are also structural inequalities between different types of former employee. These differences seem to stem from the complicated structure of the pension system itself, which comprises some 327 separate social insurance funds.

In the UK, there has been a widely reported improvement in the position of both pensioner couples and single persons in comparison with other groups in the bottom two-fifths of the income distribution. The incomes of these pensioner groups, however, have declined in comparison with changes in average income. Hidden within these statistics is an improvement in the equivalent incomes[1] of all pensioner income units, partly as a result of the wider spread of private pensions. But both single pensioners and pensioner couples are still over-represented in the bottom two-fifths of the income distribution. Moreover, older people in the UK are less well off than their counterparts in other leading industrial societies. The disposable income of households in the 65–74 age group is 76 per cent of the UK household average, compared with 93 per cent in the eight other major OECD countries (Bosanquet *et al.* 1990).

Secondly, there are wide variations between the member states in the level of protection their pension schemes provide to people on retirement. This spectrum itself comprises two related forms of inequality. On the one hand, there are variations among EU countries in the replacement ratios (retirement pension as a percentage of final earned income) of those retiring from full labour-market careers. For married men on average earnings the range stretches from Ireland and the UK at the bottom, to Greece, Italy, Portugal and Spain at the top. (The paradoxical position of the low-income southern states is explained by the fact that these 'idealized' models assumed full pension entitlements in 1989, but then only a minority of older people in the southern states were eligible for full pensions.) On the other hand, there are marked differences within and between countries in the income protection offered to those with truncated contribution records (a position more often occupied by women than men). For example, at average earnings, the difference between the full pension and reduced pension ranges from two per cent in Ireland, which has a non-contributory second pension scheme, to 46 per cent in Belgium. The citizenship-based pension systems of Scandinavia have a lower ratio between the full and reduced pension than the majority of other EU countries (Walker *et al.* 1993).

Despite the nature of the changes at the bottom of the income distribution, only a part of which may be explained by the rising incomes of older people themselves, and the static picture at the top of the income distribution, the advent of the WOOPIE – or well-off older person – was heralded in the UK in the late 1980s. This phenomenon does not appear to be related to any major shift of older people up the income distribution but, instead, to increasing inequalities among pensioners. This represents a third dimension of change in income distribution: a widening gap in living standards *within* the older population. The UK stands out among other EU countries in terms of the extent of the polarization that is occurring in pensioners' living standards.

At one extreme in the UK there is a relatively small proportion of older people – drawn from the recently retired, mainly male, higher social classes and those with a long pre-retirement experience of secure employment – who form a subset of those in the top fifth of the income distribution. They are much more likely than older people as a whole to own their own homes, to receive occupational pensions and to receive income from assets and savings. At the other extreme there is a considerably larger group (at least five times larger) who are likely to be women, older than the affluent group and less likely to have been in long-term secure employment or in the higher social classes. This group of poor older people are more likely to be reliant on national insurance (NI) pensions and income support than their affluent counterparts.

Underlying this increasing inequality is the differential rate of increases in the various components of UK pensioners' incomes. Between 1979 and 1988 social security rose by only 14 per cent in real terms, compared with 99 per cent for occupational pensions and 110 per cent for savings income. A significant part of the explanation for this differential rate of increase is the policy decision to de-index the basic pension from earnings. Thus, the level of the single person's pension has fallen from 20.4 per cent of average weekly earnings in 1979 to 16.2 per cent in 1991; for the married couples' pension, the figures are 32.7 per cent and 26 per cent respectively (House of Commons 1991).

Among the poorest older people in the UK, are at least 700,000 living on incomes *below* the income support levels. This includes a significant number of pensioners who are eligible for this means-tested social assistance benefit but who do not claim it – one in five of those eligible (Department of Health and Social Security 1989). Research suggests that this is due to a combination of factors, including the stigma attached to claiming means-tested benefits and lack of information (Townsend 1979). Certainly it is a longstanding problem that has not been overcome by periodic publicity campaigns designed to increase take-up and appears to be endemic in the means-tested nature of social assistance. Older people are particularly prone to being put off from claiming means-tested benefits.

Turning to the UK's modified State Earnings Related Pension Scheme (SERPS), it has been calculated that the net replacement ratio of the NI pension plus a SERPS addition for a person on average male earnings over a lifetime will be only 42.5 per cent (Atkinson 1991: 13). This compares with replacement ratios of 66 per cent in France and 69 per cent in Italy and 78 per cent in some UK occupational schemes. It is about one-fifth less than would have been the case under the original SERPS. Again, this suggests that policy has focused more on the future cost of pensions than on the adequacy of the pensions provided.

As for personal pensions, the problem here is that only the NI pension is assured; the second-tier component depends on the outcome of investments. As one economist has put it, 'A guarantee is replaced by a lottery' (Atkinson 1991: 21). This poses serious questions for the fate of those older people whose investments fail to yield sufficient to raise the (falling relative) value of the basic NI pension to an adequate level.

One of the main intentions of SERPS was to reduce the high reliance of older people on means-tested social assistance benefits, and the evidence suggests that it would have had a dramatic impact on poverty in old age. The recent changes in pension policy will seriously undermine the capacity of the Scheme to achieve this goal and, as a result, a significant proportion of older people are likely to be living on very low incomes well into the next century. This is particularly the case for older women. Recent research conducted for the Equal Opportunities Commission (EOC) concluded that occupational and personal pensions do not meet the needs of women. They are more likely than men to have long periods on low incomes, doing part-time work or out of the labour market while raising or caring for family members and, therefore, are disadvantaged by pension schemes linked to levels of earnings and length of service (Davies and Ward 1992; see also Groves 1992).

Thus these changes in pension policy in the UK have pre-empted concerns of the kind apparent in some other EU countries about the combined effects of demography and the maturation of pension schemes on public expenditure. The corollary is that UK pensioners are likely to remain worse off than their northern EU counterparts for the foreseeable future. Moreover, the policy of holding the basic NI pension at its 1979 (real) level while encouraging the growth of occupational and personal pensions will result in an even sharper polarization of income levels among future pensioners, with low-paid, part-time employees (predominantly women) having the poorest prospects.

The persistence of poverty and low incomes

Fourthly, despite generally rising living standards and the achievement of high replacement ratios in some member states, the EU Observatory revealed a continuing problem of poverty among a minority of older people, with the size of the minority varying considerably between countries. (Some of the human consequences of continuing poverty among older people in the EU can be found in the collection of case studies published by Eurolink Age: Webster 1992.)

Statistics on poverty among older people represent one of the key deficiencies in the information available to policy makers. This is partly due to the political sensitivity of such data and also to the longstanding controversy concerning definitions of poverty. It is unfortunate that the latest figures from Eurostat to provide comparative data for all member states (published in 1990) cover only the period 1980–5. It is very difficult, therefore, to piece together a picture of the contemporary position of older people in the EU with regard to this most sensitive of indicators of their living standards and potential for social integration. This difficulty is exacerbated by the under-representation of low-income groups in some national household and budget surveys. Also, there is the additional problem for policy makers, especially in the affluent states, that the rising living standards of the recently retired may have a disproportionate influence on the average incomes of pensioners and mask continuing pockets of poverty among older people.

Because of the lack of reliable recent comparative data and the problems associated with defining poverty, it was possible for the Observatory to take only some tentative first steps towards an evaluation of the effectiveness of the pension and wider social protection systems of member states in tackling poverty in old age, and the results should be treated with caution. Using two rather minimal national definitions of poverty among older people – the percentage living on or below social assistance levels (sometimes referred to as an 'official' definition), and the percentage living on incomes below half of average disposable earnings – EU countries were divided roughly into three groups. There are those countries with relatively low poverty rates among older people (less than ten per cent): Denmark, Germany (former FRG), Ireland and Luxembourg. Then there are those member states with median poverty rates (10–29 per cent): Belgium, France, Italy and the Netherlands. Finally there are the countries with high poverty rates among older people (30 per cent plus): Greece, Portugal, Spain and the UK. The cases of Belgium, Italy and the UK were particularly difficult to classify, though for different reasons. Belgium proved difficult because of conflicting survey data; Italy because poverty among older people is twice as high in the south of the country as in the centre–north; and the UK because the government's preferred low-income standard produces a higher poverty rate than the one based on social assistance (Walker *et al.* 1993).

In the first of these three groups, those with relatively low poverty rates, Denmark is an administrative anomaly since no statistics are kept regarding levels of poverty. However, some seven per cent of the whole of the Danish population can be said to be in poverty, defined as less than DKK1000 per month once all fixed expenses have been paid. In Luxembourg, where figures do exist, in 1986 only 6.7 per cent of older-person households lived below the official poverty line (minimal social income) and 7.4 per cent lived below 50 per cent of the average disposable equivalent income standard. However, these figures are before the introduction of a guaranteed minimum income as a result of pension reforms in 1987 and 1991 which have resulted in a halving of the poverty rates for this sector of the population. According to Callan *et al.* (1989), the relative poverty of senior citizens in Ireland has fallen dramatically, particularly since 1983. The proportion of older people living below a poverty line of 50 per cent of average earnings has declined from 24.4 per cent in 1980 to 9.7 per cent in 1987. This reduction is a result of both an increased tax burden coupled with a 17 per cent rise in social assistance (welfare) pensions over the period and the associated slow down in the growth of average earnings. Moreover, the fact that the numbers out of work doubled during this period also had a stabilizing effect upon the relative income position of older people outside the labour market.

In the second group of countries, that is, those with median rates of poverty, France is at the lower end, with only 15 per cent of people aged 65 and over receiving allowance from the means-tested minimum National Solidarity Fund (FNS) despite the old-age minimum increasing at above the inflation rate. Similarly, the Netherlands is in the lower half of this group, with 17 per cent of the population over 65 having disposable incomes on or just above the minimum levels regarded by the state as acceptable. There is also a tendency for single people over 80 to have higher rates than the rest of the population over 65.

The third group of countries, those with high levels of poverty among older people (with the exception of the UK), comprise the southern states of the Union, with less highly developed welfare systems than the northern ones. Although Italy has a more highly developed welfare system than Greece and Spain there are wide disparities in provision between the urban and rural areas. For example, the incidence of poverty is twice as high in the more rural south than the more urbanized centre–north of Italy. Among those aged 66–75, the poverty rate (as measured by those with disposable incomes below 50 per cent of the average) is 34.1 per cent in the south and 14.9 per cent in the north, while for those aged over 75 the figures are 41.5 per cent and 22.6 per cent respectively. Indeed, Florea *et al.* (in translation) (1992: 34) suggest that:

> Particularly in the southern and depressed regions of the country, the risk of poverty spreads to become a permanent and structural reality for a wide segment of the ageing population.

In the case of Portugal, little or no statistical evidence is available on the levels of poverty among older people. However, a recent family budget survey demonstrated that 49.6 per cent of pensioners under the age of 75 have incomes below half the national average net income, while for those over 75 the figure is 68.9 per cent. In Greece, where no means-tested state minimum income for pensioners exists, there is a large number of mainly ex-farmers who live on pensions with an average value of one-sixth of the minimum wage. Yet evidence from the Observatory indicates that one-third of the population in poverty comprises people aged 65 and over, with 26 per cent of the 65–74-years-olds and 42 per cent of those over 75 in poverty.

Although data are not generally available, another sensitive indicator of living standards is the ownership of consumer durables. Evidence from the Observatory indicates that, on the one hand (with the exception of Denmark), there are differences in the ownership of consumer durables between older people and younger adults (not surprisingly, these tend to be widest in countries with the largest concentrations of poverty in old age), while, on the other hand, there are inequalities among older people between the younger and older age groups.

The 'old poor' and 'new poor'

Research over the past decade on poverty has identified a decline in the proportion of older people in poverty and a concomitant rise in the proportion of families with children. The main cause of this change has been the increase in unemployment across Europe together with the general rise in the level of pensions and a higher incidence of low pay in some countries. These changes have resulted in the distinction being made between 'old poor' and 'new poor'.

There are two important policy issues arising from these changes in the composition of poverty. Will substantial falls in the levels of unemployment lead to a reduction in the significance of these 'new poor' and will the 'old poor' return to the bottom of the income distribution, as is the case in the UK? If this is to be prevented, social policy will clearly have to be directed to both the creation of employment opportunities as well as the provision of adequate social protection for older people. As the living standards of older people are susceptible to changes made within public policy, policy makers have to bear these facts in mind.

Despite these shifts in the patterns of poverty throughout Europe, old age is still a significant indicator of poverty and low incomes, even within the most successful of Europe's welfare regimes. Moreover, and as we indicated earlier in this chapter, poverty in old age is increasingly becoming feminized. Thus the close attention that has been paid by policy makers to aggregate data and the newly retired has to be balanced by acknowledging the fact that they have overlooked the persistence of long-term poverty among older persons, who are more likely to be women.

Therefore, throughout the Union, retirement and the receipt of a pension are still associated with low incomes relative to those in employment. However, there are major variations between countries in the Union in both the degree of inequality and the size of the relatively deprived older population. What can be achieved by concerted social and economic policies is exemplified by France. Over the past 20 years the position of older people has seen considerable improvement compared with those in employment. For example, from 1970 to 1985 the real value of the retirement pensions had risen by 1.8 times and the old-age minimum by 2.6 times, compared with a rise of earnings over the same period of 1.4 times. By 1989 official research had demonstrated that older households on average had the same standard of living as that of households consisting of two economically active people with two children.

In all EU countries, employment income plays a relatively small part in contributing to the living standards of older people, although there are considerable variations between countries. In recent discussions about the future of pensions systems, the idea of extending the portion of the older population that remains economically active, either in full- or in part-time employment, has received some serious consideration by governments (Chapter 5).

To summarize the main trends and policy issues concerning living standards that have been outlined so far in this chapter (based on the findings of the EU Observatory):

1 the living standards of older people are rising, particularly among those in their third age (aged 50–74);
2 there are wide variations between countries in pensioners' living standards;
3 poverty and low incomes persist among a significant minority of older people in most countries;
4 the incidence of poverty is higher among older women, particularly widows, in most EU countries;
5 income inequalities are growing among pensioners, often resulting from income maintenance and pensions policies themselves and, associated with this, particular gender-based and generational inequalities.

Subjective perceptions of living standards

What has been discussed thus far in this chapter may seem remote from what older people themselves feel about the levels and adequacy of their own incomes. This is where the results from the Eurobarometer surveys are able to make a major contribution. Results from the survey of both the public's and older people's opinions often contradict the policy statements from EU governments. When the general public were asked an open-ended question about the main problems facing older people, two issues were mentioned more than any others: financial difficulties and loneliness. Of the two, financial problems were more frequently mentioned, with an average of just under half of those sampled saying that they regarded this as the main problem facing older people in their country. However, there were wide variations between countries, as indicated in Figure 4.1.

It is interesting that when these responses are divided according to age, there is a slightly greater tendency for younger people to put financial problems first. For example, among those aged 25–44, just over half indicated that financial difficulties was the main problem, whereas approximately 45 per cent of those over 55 identified it as the main problem. Older people were more likely than

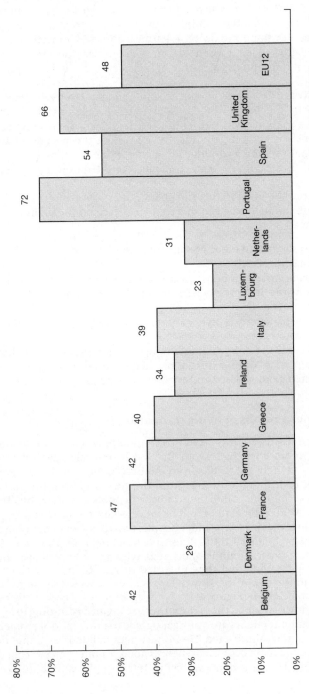

Figure 4.1 Proportions saying that the main problem facing older people in their country is not having enough to live on or financial difficulties.

those aged 15–24 to say loneliness or isolation is the main problem facing older people: 36 per cent against an average of 44 per cent in other age groups.

Turning to the special survey of older people themselves, they were asked to describe their current financial situation according to five different classifications. The results shown in Table 4.1 demonstrate that the financial position of the majority of the respondents could be described as 'getting by with care'. These subjective opinions coincide with the objective evidence on income levels, outlined earlier, that despite rising living standards there exists a continuing problem of poverty and low incomes among older people. In most countries only a minority of older people regarded themselves as comfortable or very comfortable financially. The exceptions are Denmark, the Netherlands and Luxembourg, where nearly 76 per cent, 67 per cent and 52 per cent respectively regarded themselves as 'comfortable' or 'very comfortable'. It is significant that in two of these, Denmark and the Netherlands, receipt of a pension is based wholly or substantially upon citizenship.

Yet it is important to note that, by a large majority, older people regard themselves as financially secure. Of course there were variations between member states but, overall, more than seven out of ten older Europeans said they were financially secure. So, regardless of the objective situation, there was no sign of widespread subjective feelings of financial insecurity on the part of older people. However, British social gerontology researchers have long been aware of an apparent paradox whereby older people who, by objective criteria, are suffering poverty and deprivation may nonetheless express, subjectively, satisfaction with their living standards. It may be, therefore, that this paradox is common to all EU countries and further research is required to see if this is true.

The majority and the minority were then asked, in turn, what makes them feel financially secure or insecure. Dealing with the majority first, by far the most important factor overall was the public pension system (seven out of ten nominations). Looking beyond the EU average, this held good for all individual countries except two: Greece, where a slim majority said that their house or property was the main source of their financial security; and the UK, where the same factor came first but by a larger, though still small, majority. Older people in the UK ranked the state pension system lower than those in any other EU country and far lower than other northern EU states (48 per cent compared with 90 per cent in Germany and 75 per cent in France).

The role of the public sector in creating a sense of financial security among senior citizens was not rivalled in any country by employers' or private pensions, with the exception of the UK, where it received nearly the same level of support. Looking at the average for the EU as a whole, private and occupational pensions ranked sixth in importance. Ahead of them were housing/property (most important in Ireland, Greece and the UK and least so in the Netherlands); next personal savings (highest score in Germany and lowest in Spain); then good health (most important in France and least important in Portugal and Spain); and then family support (highest in Greece and lowest in the Netherlands and Denmark). In this last respect the differences between the north and south of the Union were striking. The proportion nominating family support as the basis of financial security in Greece was nearly eight times the proportion in the Netherlands, four times that in Germany and twice that in the UK.

Table 4.1 Financial situation of older people (older people only)

	EU12	B	D	F	G	GR	IRL	I	L	NL	P	SP	UK
Very comfortable	3.5	2.4	18.3	1.8	1.1	0.8	4.3	6.1	8.9	5.2	0.7	2.5	5.5
Comfortable	32.6	31.3	57.5	34.5	18.6	16.5	36.0	44.0	58.1	46.8	22.8	31.5	39.0
I have to be careful, but I get by	51.4	56.2	22.1	52.7	71.6	32.0	45.5	39.5	24.5	41.3	45.8	38.3	47.7
I have trouble making ends meet	8.9	6.7	1.2	7.1	7.5	34.1	10.8	6.6	4.5	5.2	17.8	20.7	5.1
Things are very difficult	2.9	1.2	0.9	3.5	0.4	16.2	2.4	2.6	0.4	0.8	11.6	5.6	2.5
Don't know	0.8	2.2	0	0.4	0.7	0.4	0.9	1.2	3.6	0.8	1.4	1.4	0.1

The public sector was the main ingredient in pensioners' financial security but it was the leading one, by far, in causing insecurity as well. Thus, some seven out of ten of those older people in the EU who said they felt financially insecure blamed the low level of state benefits and pensions. The highest proportions (over 80 per cent) were in Greece and Luxembourg and the lowest were in Denmark and the UK (56–8 per cent). Next in line with regard to financial insecurity was the level of savings being too small, then poor health followed by private or occupational pensions being too small.

Older people were asked if they would have liked to have made additional pension contributions or savings when they were younger, and only a minority said they would not (29 per cent). Not surprisingly, answers to this question were related to those concerning financial security. Thus, in Denmark, a large majority said they did not, while in Portugal it was only a tiny minority. An obvious question which follows from this is, if an individual wanted to make additional contributions, could they have afforded to? In all but two countries, Denmark and Belgium, the answer was no. Across the EU as a whole, three-fifths of older people would have liked to have made additional contributions or savings but two-thirds of them said that they could not have afforded to do so. The biggest gaps between aspirations and ability to pay were, predictably, in Greece, Portugal and Spain but also in the former GDR.

How much is enough?

In order to gauge the attitudes of the citizens of the 12 EU states, a number of benchmark questions were asked in the Eurobarometer surveys about the adequacy of pensions and the levels of income older people should expect to live on. Those in the general population survey who had retired were asked whether the pensions (public and private) they receive are adequate. The results are shown in Figure 4.2. As can be seen, the Union divided into three groups: those countries where a large majority of older people regard their pensions as adequate (Denmark, Germany, Luxembourg and the Netherlands); those where opinion was split on adequacy versus inadequacy (Belgium, France, Ireland, Italy, Spain and the UK); and those where large majorities said pensions are inadequate (Greece and Portugal). This evidence is not concerned with objective measures but, viewed from the perspective of those on the receiving end, the EU's pension systems clearly cannot be regarded as entirely successful in terms of their adequacy. It is only in four member states that older people seem to be mainly satisfied with their pension.

The results of a second question to pensioners in the main Eurobarometer survey seem to indicate a relatively high level of frustrated aspirations and perhaps even latent resentment over the level of pensions people had accrued when in employment. The survey asked them to take into account the contributions they had made during their working lives and then to say whether the pension they now receive allows them to lead the life they would like to lead. Only just over one in eight were definitely positive in their response to this question, the most certain being in Denmark (34 per cent) and Luxembourg (39 per cent). Adding together those who said 'yes, definitely' and those who said 'probably' there were what we might call satisfied

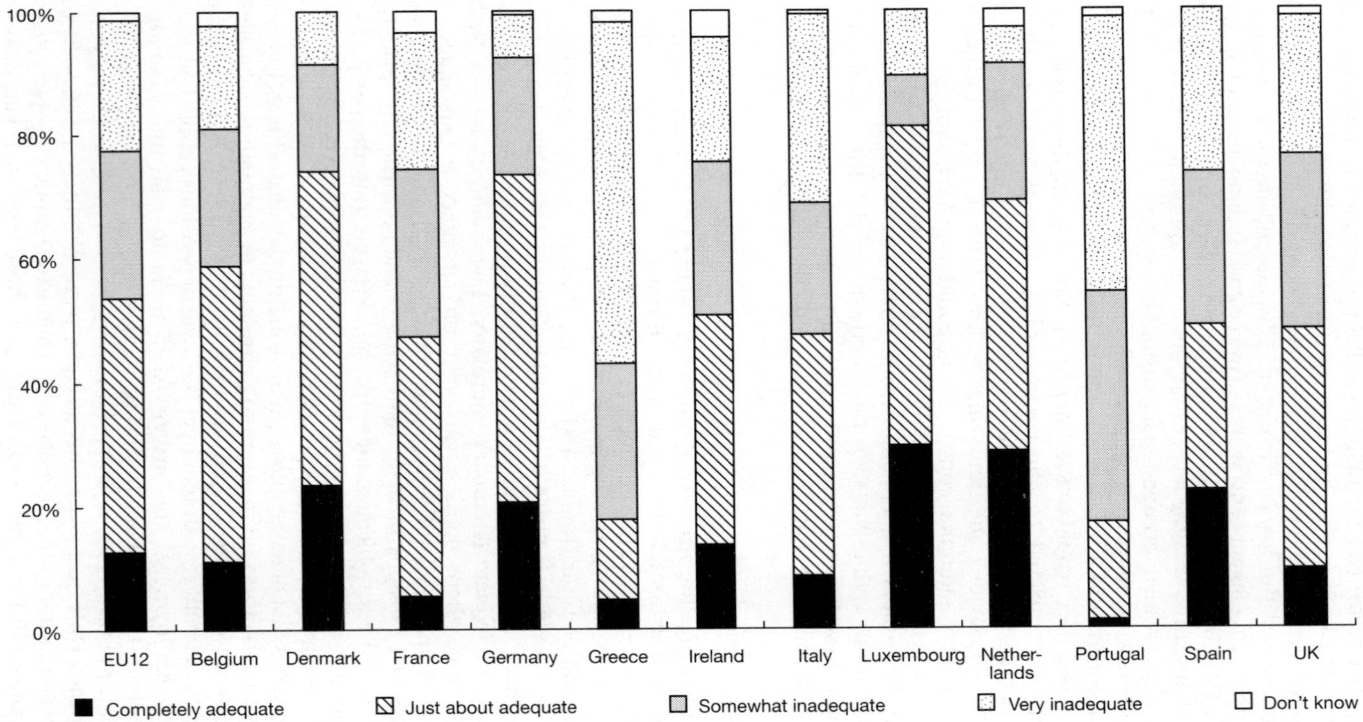
100%
80%
60%
40%
20%
0%
EU12
Belgium
Denmark
France
Germany
Greece
Ireland
Italy
Luxembourg
Nether-
lands
Portugal
Spain
UK
Completely adequate
Just about adequate
Somewhat inadequate
Very inadequate
Don't know

Figure 4.2 The adequacy of pensions (older people only).

majorities in Belgium, Denmark, Luxembourg and the Netherlands. Thus in Denmark, Luxembourg and the Netherlands there appeared to be a high level of contentment on the part of pensioners with the level of the pensions they receive as both a source of income and a well earned reward for a working life. The countries in which older people were most definite that their pensions do not produce the living standards they would like after a lifetime's contributions were, in descending order: Greece (66 per cent), Portugal (56 per cent), Italy and Spain (42 per cent) and the UK (41 per cent).

In the main Eurobarometer survey the opinion of the general public about the appropriate level of income that should be provided by the state to older people was sought. Here we are talking about the *minimum* level of guaranteed income. The results, in Figure 4.3, provide substantial backing for the conclusion drawn from Figure 3.1, that there is solid support in the EU for the public provision of a decent standard of living for older people. This is a conclusion with immense significance for policy makers. As the graph shows, there is hardly any support for the 'Beveridge' subsistence option. Fairness proved the most attractive choice in Denmark and the Netherlands (which may have something to do with the fact that these two countries have public pension systems that are based wholly or substantially on citizenship rather than contributions through employment). However, it was the 'Bismarck option' of earnings equivalence (i.e. for a pension set close to or at the average working wage) that was favoured by majorities in most countries. It is interesting to note that there is little variation in opinions concerning minimum state pensions by either age or sex. The average figures according to age are shown in Table 4.2.

Paying for pensions

As we saw in Chapter 3, there was very strong support for the maintenance of the intergenerational social contract whereby taxes and contributions levied on those in employment pay for the pensions of those in retirement – what is sometimes referred to as pay-as-you-go. The previous discussion of the adequacy or inadequacy of pensions raises the question of how they should be financed. Since issues concerning the level of pensions and their financing are intertwined, though rarely considered together in social surveys, a question linking the two was put to the general public in each country.

The results, shown in Table 4.3 by country and averaged in Figure 4.4, reveal a clear distinction between the general public's opinion on the pensions/taxation equation in those countries with pension levels in the top half of the EU league as compared with those in the bottom half. The former are more likely to have said that pension levels are about right or that they are too low but will have to stay at that level, while the latter are more likely to have said that they are too low and should be raised even if this means increasing contributions or taxes. The stark difference between the former FRG and GDR was significant in this respect. On the contrary, the minuscule proportions in every member state of people saying that pensions are too high was striking. It is also noteworthy that there was hardly any variation between age groups in responses to this question, with the exception of those aged 15–24, who were

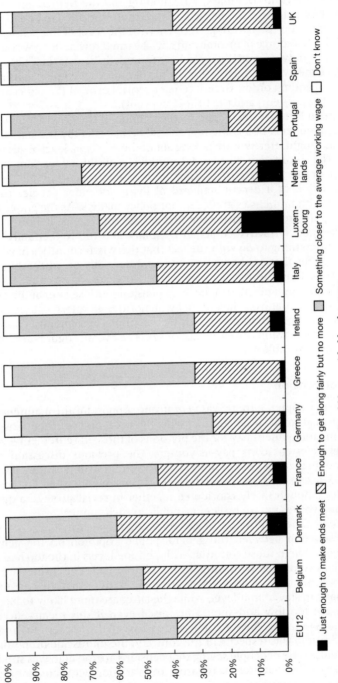

Figure 4.3 The level of minimum resources that should be provided by the state.

Legend:
- ■ Just enough to make ends meet
- ▨ Enough to get along fairly but no more
- ▥ Something closer to the average working wage
- □ Don't know

Table 4.2 Responses to question 'What level of minimum income should be provided by the state?' according to age (percentages)

	15–24	*25–34*	*35–44*	*45–54*	*55–64*	*65+*
Just enough to make ends meet	4	4	5	4	4	3
Enough to get along fairly but not more	41	34	32	35	33	35
Something closer to the average wage for people still in work	50	58	60	58	60	58
Don't know	5	4	3	3	3	4

significantly less likely than older groups to say pensions are too low and should be raised regardless of the consequences for taxes and contributions.

Related to the question of pension financing is the issue of who should be responsible for pension provision: the state, employers or individual workers? In most EU countries a majority of the public thought that pensions should be provided mainly by the public authorities and financed from contributions or taxes. On average just under half (49 per cent) of the sample of the whole population of the EU was of this opinion. The countries that deviated from this majority position were Germany (though the former GDR was in favour and the former FRG against – 55 per cent compared with 33 per cent), the Netherlands and the UK (though only just: 48 per cent). In the case of Germany the preferred alternative was a pension provided by employers and financed mainly from their own and their employees' contributions. In the Netherlands and the UK opinions were split between this method and private contracts between individual workers and pension companies, though it must be said that only in the Netherlands did the proportion favouring the private provision of pensions exceed 15 per cent and, overall, this approach was supported by only one in ten of respondents across the EU.

Pensions or concessions?

The issue of whether or not senior citizens should pay reduced prices for certain staple items, such as electricity and transport, is a contentious one. For many years several EU countries have provided goods and services free or at a reduced price for older people. The most common items are bus and rail passes and home helps. However, several countries have gone further in providing benefits in kind specifically for older people. Examples include Italy, where since 1989 those in receipt of an old-age pension have been exempt from health care fees. In France there are free or reduced-price leisure activities, holidays and home helps. In both Denmark and the UK older people obtain health services free at the point of use. Research by the EU's Observatory suggests that Denmark has the most extensive provision of such subsidies. The

Table 4.3 Pensions and taxation: more or less?

	B	D	F	FRG	GDR	G	GR	IRL	I	L	NL	P	SP	UK
Pensions are too low and should be raised even if this means raising taxes	36.3	30.1	27.0	20.3	48.6	26.2	66.3	29.0	53.8	28.1	16.8	73.7	66.8	56.6
Pensions are too low but cannot be raised because taxes should not be increased	34.1	36.3	42.9	42.8	27.8	39.6	14.1	33.6	20.5	16.8	25.0	17.2	14.4	20.7
Pensions are too high and should be reduced	1.7	0.2	1.8	1.1	0.0	0.8	0.3	0.6	0.6	2.3	0.2	0.9	0.4	0.3
Pensions are about right	19.5	29.7	22.1	26.8	15.9	24.5	5.2	18.1	8.4	40.0	41.6	2.4	7.6	14.9
Don't know	8.4	3.6	7.2	9.0	7.7	8.8	14.0	18.7	16.7	12.9	16.5	5.8	10.8	7.5

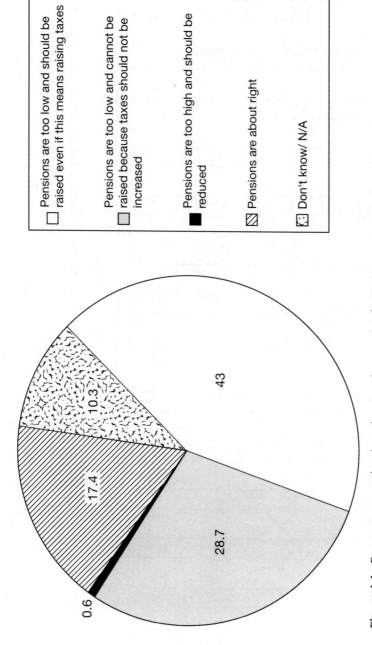

Figure 4.4 Responses to pensions/taxation equation question for EU12 (percentages) (see Table 4.3 also).

Pensions are too low and should be raised even if this means raising taxes

Pensions are too low and cannot be raised because taxes should not be increased

Pensions are too high and should be reduced

Pensions are about right

Don't know/ N/A

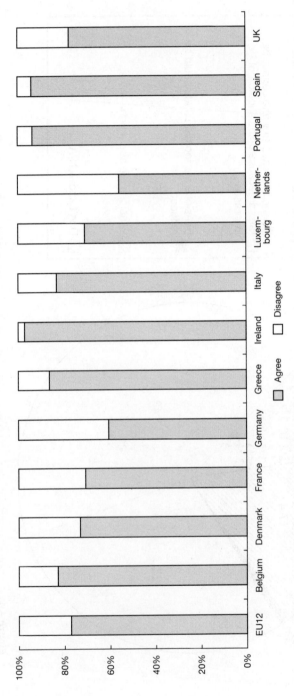

Figure 4.5 Responses to the preposition 'Elderly people should be given reduced prices for things like gas, electricity, telephone and transport' ('don't know' not shown).

EU bus and rail pass for senior citizens has been the subject of a long campaign by organizations working for older people and members of the European Parliament. On the other hand it may be argued that such concessions run the risk of conveying a sort of second-class status on older people (Chapter 3).

A recent study has attempted to quantify such benefits in kind in various countries, including some EU countries, and was one of the first comparative studies to do so (Whiteford and Kennedy 1995). This analysis concentrated upon the non-cash income resulting from health, education, owner-occupied housing and the imputed income from liquid assets (shares, savings, etc.). However, perhaps owing to the limited nature of the conceptualization of this 'non-cash' income the researchers concluded that the 'determinants of living standards are complex', with considerable variety and complexity between different countries. Their conclusion that the 'total package of resources available' should be taken into account when assessing the living standards of older people echoes many previous discussions of living standards in old age (see for example Townsend 1979).

In order to highlight the main policy issue in this difficult area it was decided to ask the general public whether or not they support the idea of older people getting reduced prices for things like gas, electricity, telephone and transport. Across the whole of the EU the support was overwhelming, adding further to the already strong impression of a general sense of older people's deservingness in the eyes of the people of Europe (see Figure 4.5). As the graph shows, nearly three out of four people aged 15 and over agreed, and of these well over half of them did so strongly. The strongest expressions of agreement were in Ireland, Portugal, Spain and the UK, and the strongest disagreement was found in Germany and the Netherlands. There is some slight hint here that the countries with the best pension systems in the EU (in terms of the level of subjective satisfaction of pensioners) were the least likely to favour concessions.

But what about older people themselves? How do they view the pensions/ concessions dilemma? First of all, when we break down the general public's views by age, we find that those aged 65 and over were more likely than younger groups to favour reduced prices (51 per cent compared with 35 per cent of those aged 15–24 and 40 per cent aged 25–34). Secondly, in the special survey of senior citizens we posed the question in the form of a choice between money in the form of a pension, on the one hand, and on the other, reduced prices and concessions. If an older person responded 'both of these' then that was recorded. The results, shown in Figure 4.6, indicate a strong preference for money to spend as older people themselves choose. This was not really surprising, but important nonetheless, not least because this is the first opportunity that older people had to express an opinion on the subject simultaneously in each member state of the EU.

Looking forward to retirement

Finally in this chapter we report the results of some Eurobarometer questions designed to see what the general public thinks the future has in store for them as they grow older. Respondents were asked to agree or disagree with the statement 'I am worried about how adequate my pension will be when I

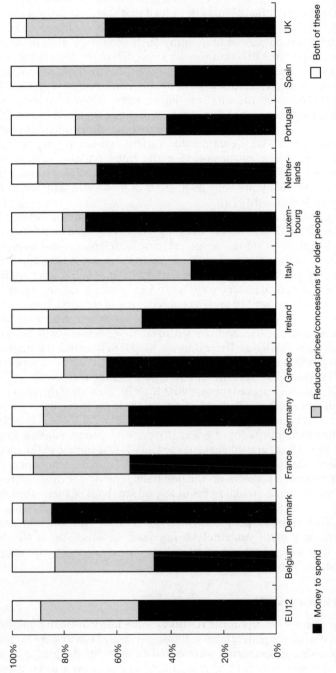

Figure 4.6 How to support older people: money or concessions? (Older people only). The exact question was: 'The government has different ways of supporting elderly people. Some say that they should have the money in the form of a pension to spend as they wish, whilst others say they should benefit from reduced prices or concessions that apply to them. If you had to choose one of these, which would it be?' (Don't know response not shown.)

■ Money to spend   □ Reduced prices/concessions for older people   □ Both of these retire/is, now that I am retired'. Their responses revealed widespread concern in all EU countries. Three-fifths of the whole European population agreed strongly or slightly and, as far as individual countries are concerned, France, Greece and Portugal had the highest levels of agreement. Those that appeared to be least worried were in Denmark, Luxembourg and the Netherlands. So it seems that financial security in old age may have some connection with the degree of optimism with which those of working age view the future. Looking at the results according to age it was the middle aged (35–44-year-olds) who were most worried about the adequacy of their future pensions.

There is also quite a high level of pessimism among the general public about how far the pensions contract will be honoured in the future. Thus when asked whether people will get less pension for their contributions in the future, just over one half of the public said yes. There has been much debate in recent years in all EU countries (and many others beyond the EU too) about the cost implications of population ageing. In some countries this debate has been couched in extreme and alarmist terms, such as the 'burden' of pensions and the 'threat' posed by pensioners to economic progress; it is not surprising therefore if the general public echoes this pessimism to some extent (Walker 1990; Myles and Quadagno 1991).

In France more than three-quarters of the public thought that the pensions contract would be modified adversely, and in Belgium, Denmark and the Netherlands it was three-fifths. Only in Greece and Portugal were there larger numbers saying that they did *not* expect older people to get less pensions for their contributions in the future. Also in Greece, Ireland, Italy, Portugal and Spain between one-fifth and one-third responded that they did not know what would happen, which underlies the general sense of uncertainty about the future of pensions in some countries.

In a similar vein we wondered if people thought that, given the increasing numbers of older people, those in employment would have to retire later. A majority thought not (54 per cent). The countries most likely to say yes were Germany (mainly the former FRG) and the Netherlands. The pension reforms introduced in Germany at the start of 1992 were aimed, in part, at a phased increase in retirement age, so German public opinion may to some extent be reflecting what is happening in policy terms. No such change has taken place in the Netherlands, though there have been public discussions about the cost of pensions. In both France and Italy official proposals to alter the pensions contract have been made recently but these did not seem to have filtered through to public opinion.

Finally, the issue of the ability of the welfare state to cope with increasing numbers of older people was put to the test of public opinion by asking whether or not the welfare state will continue to grow and take care of older people better than now. Again, quite a high level of pessimism and uncertainty was uncovered in some countries. Overall only just under one in three were confident enough in the future of the welfare state to say yes. Half replied negatively and the remaining one in five did not know. The largest concentrations of pessimism were in Denmark, France, the former FRG (nearly double the number in the former GDR) and the Netherlands. Perhaps the general public in those countries with some of the highest pension levels in the

EU were saying that they did not think it will last; alternatively, we could interpret their responses as meaning they do not think it is possible to improve on the present superior position in their country.

Note

1 This refers to income (usually household income) which is adjusted to account for variation in household size and composition so as to allow comparison. It is therefore an attempt to reflect the gains and losses associated with different forms and types of household.

5

Employment and older workers

The changing character of old age discussed in Chapter 2 is partly reflected in the transition from fixed-age retirement to more flexible forms of exit from the labour force. Even though older people are living longer and healthier lives there is a universal tendency towards the shortening of the period spent in paid employment (Kohli *et al.* 1991; Guillemard 1993). Unfortunately for many older workers this 'flexibility' has been down the age range only, and early exit has often been largely beyond their control. This chapter considers the complex set of issues concerning older workers and presents evidence from both the Eurobarometer surveys, the Observatory country reports, and the summary produced by Guillemard (1993).

Within the EU, particularly over the last 20 years, greater numbers of older people are leaving paid employment before their normal retirement age, generally at the age of 55 (see Table 5.1). This trend is not only a pan-European phenomenon but is common to all industrialized countries (with the exception of Sweden and Japan), though the rates of decline vary considerably (Guillemard 1993). The measure used by Guillemard (1993) to quantify these shifts was the 'employment rate' rather than the 'activity rate'. She argued that it was more relevant since it represents the proportions in paid work and excludes the unemployed. This exclusion of the unemployed is important in the context of older people since most older people who are unemployed have little hope of returning to paid work. Furthermore, unemployment has become a significant method of early exit from the labour force for older people and particularly for older men. Additionally she documents the evidence only for men, suggesting that the trends for older women are masked by the rapid entry of women into paid work and, further, she suggests that this entry was not 'over identical timescales nor in the same measure in the different countries of Europe' (Guillemard 1993: 70). Because of this, interpretation of labour market activity is particularly difficult she argues, and is the reason why

Table 5.1 Evolution of percentage employment rates for men over 55 and women over 50 by age groups in the 12 EU countries (1983–94)

Men

		B	DK	F	G	GR	IRL	I	L	NL	P	SP	UK
55–9	1983	60.9	77.4	60.3	77.6	76.4	76.5	71.1	52.5	65.3	74.7	79.1	75.8
	1986	54.2	78.3	57.3	73.9	73.7	71.6	67.2	56.5	–	72.1	67.9	73.3
	1988	48.1	78.8	56.3	72.2	72.4	69.9	66.4	54.6	63.4	69.9	66.6	72.6
	1990	48.4	81.6	56.2	73.9	70.7	69.6	66.4	62.8	63.6	73.5	69.4	74.9
	1992	48.7	75.7	58.1	67.2	70.8	66.7	63.9	53.3	60.9	68.8	66.7	69.5
	1994	48.6	75.1	55.9	63.9	71.0	67.8	59.3	51.3	59.3	68.9	60.7	67.3
60–4	1983	27.4	48.3	28.2	38.3	58.2	63.3	35.9	19.5	34.2	62.8	60.4	52.5
	1986	22.4	52.6	22.0	30.8	51.7	57.3	36.7	16.1	–	53.5	45.6	48.1
	1988	19.4	51.7	19.4	31.7	49.2	55.0	36.4	18.0	25.1	53.7	44.0	49.1
	1990	18.9	48.6	16.0	32.9	45.5	50.4	34.5	22.8	21.7	54.2	43.2	49.4
	1992	20.2	45.8	13.5	28.5	45.9	52.1	33.1	15.7	21.4	55.4	43.0	47.5
	1994	17.3	40.9	12.5	26.1	45.5	50.6	29.6	15.1	21.0	52.2	38.0	45.1
55–64	1983	47.7	63.1	46.0	60.2	68.8	70.3	55.3	38.0	50.5	–	–	64.3
	1986	38.8	65.8	40.6	55.4	64.0	64.6	52.7	39.6	–	63.2	57.5	61.1
	1988	34.4	65.5	38.7	54.1	61.6	62.7	52.0	39.7	44.1	62.2	55.9	61.1
	1990	34.3	65.6	37.0	54.3	58.4	60.2	50.9	42.9	44.0	64.6	56.9	63.3
	1992*	34.7	61.5	35.9	49.5	58.6	59.8	48.9	40.0	42.2	62.0	55.0	58.7
65–9	1983	5.1	26.4	7.9	10.2	34.1	31.6	15.0	(10.2)	5.3	–	20.7	13.0
	1986	5.5	26.0	7.1	8.5	26.8	28.3	15.5	(4.5)	–	30.3	10.9	11.7
	1988	4.2	25.9	6.1	7.4	24.1	26.8	13.8	(4.2)	10.0	30.6	7.5	11.3
	1990	3.3	27.4	5.1	8.6	21.4	25.7	12.8	(5.5)	9.7	31.5	7.4	13.5
	1992	3.9	26.0	5.2	6.9	21.2	25.7	12.0	–	11.1	28.5	7.0	14.1
	1994	2.3	3.8	2.5	4.3	11.7	16.0	6.2	2.1	5.8	20.6	2.9	7.3

Women

		B	DK	F	G	GR	IRL	I	L	NL	P	SP	UK
50–54	1983	26.1	63.8	52.7	45.2	35.6	24.6	29.7	20.1	25.9	–	–	60.8
	1986	26.5	68.1	53.2	47.4	38.1	23.3	31.2	25.1	–	42.9	23.7	62.1
	1988	25.8	72.6	53.7	47.9	37.9	24.3	30.8	24.0	33.3	45.9	24.7	62.0
	1990	28.6	72.9	55.3	53.8	36.3	25.5	31.7	26.9	36.0	47.6	25.5	65.2
	1992	31.8	74.1	57.1	59.5	35.1	27.9	33.4	30.6	39.9	51.9	28.7	65.7
55–59	1983	15.7	50.2	37.2	37.5	29.5	20.6	19.5	17.9	17.2	–	–	47.4
	1986	16.7	57.3	36.4	35.9	29.9	18.6	19.9	19.0	–	33.5	21.0	48.6
	1988	14.6	55.9	37.4	36.3	31.4	19.2	20.4	17.1	21.7	36.3	21.0	49.1
	1990	14.7	57.6	37.6	38.7	28.0	20.6	19.3	18.0	22.9	37.9	21.5	51.9
	1992	17.2	61.4	38.0	36.1	26.0	21.3	18.8	21.0	25.1	42.2	21.4	52.1
	1994	20.4	57.1	38.8	37.6	26.5	23.4	18.6	19.0	27.4	41.4	20.8	51.7
60–64	1983	6.0	28.0	16.6	12.1	19.9	16.5	9.0	10.2	7.7	–	–	19.7
	1986	4.2	29.2	14.7	10.5	20.9	12.1	9.5	7.5	–	23.6	14.8	18.0
	1988	3.8	22.9	14.2	10.3	22.0	11.8	9.9	7.4	7.2	26.0	15.8	18.6
	1990	4.0	26.9	11.8	11.6	19.7	13.8	10.0	9.5	8.3	23.7	14.6	21.8
	1992	5.0	24.6	11.3	9.2	17.4	12.6	8.6	9.8	6.3	27.1	15.3	22.8
	1994	4.9	20.8	11.3	8.4	18.5	13.6	8.0	7.5	7.2	24.9	15.0	24.7

Note: ( ) indicates unreliable data, sample size too small.
Sources: Guillemard 1993, Table 3.2; *Eurostat Labour Force Survey 1992* (1994), Table 6; unpublished data from Eurostat Labour Force Survey 1994, Eurostat.
* = Authors' own calculations.

her comparisons are based upon the male population. However, although we agree with much of this argument we felt it appropriate to include some information on older women (see Table 5.1) if only for comparison. We also provide a summary of the different shifts noted for women later in this chapter.

The Netherlands and France have experienced the sharpest falls in employment rates among men aged 55–64 (45 per cent and 43 per cent respectively) between 1971 and 1991. In Germany, Ireland, Spain and the UK there was a 30 per cent reduction in the employment rate of this group over the same period. It is only in Denmark, Greece and Portugal that employment rates among older workers have declined relatively modestly (see also Moore *et al.* 1994).

Over the same 20-year period there has been a corresponding shift away from public pensions systems being the principal mechanism through which an individual exits from working life. Guillemard (1993) suggests that if the analysis is refined on the basis of quinquennial age groups then paid working life for men after age 65 no longer exists in the 12 countries of the EU she considered. She qualifies this statement by suggesting that there may still be some levels of activity in Ireland, Portugal, Greece and Denmark, to which we may now also add Sweden. This is largely attributable to the large agricultural sector as well as to higher retirement ages in the two Scandinavian countries.

With the development of pension systems, the age of 65 (the age most commonly used for entitlement to pension rights) became the age at which labour market inactivity commenced. However, since the mid-1970s there has been a development of this transition being fixed at younger and younger ages. First, the employment rate fell for the 60–4-year-olds and during the 1980s this moved down the age range to the 55–9 age group. Such rapid and consistent drops in employment rates cannot be explained by the maturing of pension schemes (Guillemard 1993).

The 'down-sizing' of the workforce during this period, which was associated with economic recession throughout Europe, has not been accommodated by making younger workers redundant but rather by selecting older people for redundancy (see for example Westergaard *et al.* 1989). This was despite special employment protection for this age group (e.g. in the Netherlands). Thus exit from working life now takes place more often before any possibility for entitlement to a public-sector pension. Yet many countries in the Union (e.g. the UK, Germany, France and Italy) are raising the ages at which entitlement to such pensions is possible.

Evidence from the Observatory underlines these findings. For example, in Germany in 1988, 18.3 per cent entered the pension scheme at age 65 and 18.4 per cent took advantage of flexible retirement at 63. In total only 36 per cent went directly from paid work to a retirement pension. The remainder had ceased work by using other protection arrangements: 38.1 per cent by the Invalidity Insurance Scheme, 12.5 per cent by being declared as unfit to work, and 12.6 per cent through unemployment. The latter categories allow receipt of a public pension at age 60. In Ireland, although employment rates for 55–64-year-olds are relatively high at 60 per cent, evidence from Whelan and Whelan (1988) indicated that only 25 per cent of the newly retired took retirement at 65 years. Manual workers were shown by the same study to retire earlier, with one in four withdrawing from work before 60.

Of the 12 member states at the time of the Observatory report, only Greece, Portugal and Italy were exceptions to this phenomenon, in that their retirement pension systems continued to determine the boundary between labour market activity and inactivity. Italy is the best example, since its statutory retirement age is set at 60 for men and 55 for women, below the European norm. Thus the activity rates for older workers is low and has fallen only gradually. Moreover, some private-sector pension schemes allow receipt of a pension following contributions being paid for a minimum number of years no matter what age is achieved. This can be as low as 30 years. Thus in 1989, 45.5 per cent of men were entitled to a pension when younger than the norm, against 42.2 per cent at the normal age and 12.5 per cent after the normal age. Early retirement is therefore the main mechanism for transition to retirement for men in Italy (see Calcoen and Greiner 1992).

However, although old-age pensions and insurance are no longer the main mechanisms allowing passage from paid work to retirement, particularly for men, new public and private forms of social protection are becoming increasingly important. Predominant among these are invalidity and un-employment insurance. Generally the conditions for receipt of these two forms of mainly social transfers have been relaxed and/or broadened (with some notable exceptions, e.g. the new job seeker's allowance and incapacity benefit in the UK). We outline the use of this mechanism below when we consider the UK case in more detail. The criteria for receipt of unemployment insurance have been constantly relaxed as a means of encouraging early exit in many countries (e.g. Germany, Denmark and Ireland). In Germany and the Netherlands economic criteria allowing the employment of disabled workers on the local labour market have been added to a medical test determining incapacity to work. In this way a partial inability to undertake some forms of paid work is now recognized as being sufficient to allow entitlement to benefit and allows withdrawal from the labour market.

Added to these mechanisms there has been a specific policy shift to allow older workers to leave the labour market through the use of early retirement compensation schemes. As we noted previously, this is often associated with encouragement of the replacement of older workers by younger workers. There are several such schemes, for example the Job Release Scheme in the UK, the contract for early retirement solidarity in France, early retirement in Germany and early retirement solidarity in Luxembourg. These tend to rely upon unemployment insurance or public employment intervention funds and are financed partly or totally by public money. Alternatively, employers may finance them by establishing policies encouraging early retirement (e.g. in Spain and Portugal) or through a framework of institutional arrangements created by collective bargaining, as with the 'voluntary' early exit scheme (Vroegtijdige Uittreding (VUT)) in the Netherlands.

Yet again there are differences in the findings between the north and south of the Union. Although invalidity benefits have been used occasionally in southern countries (i.e. Spain, Italy and Portugal), their role has not been as dominant as in the northern countries. The most frequently used methods have been early retirement as a result of modernization and reconversion of the industrial sector and have been jointly funded by the state and employers.

However, Guillemard (1993) notes that few governments have been able to get agreements with employers to bear the major portion of the expenditure for early retirement schemes. Thus the German Early Retirement Act had this aim in mind, but because of its unpopularity it failed to become a reality. It is in the Netherlands, with the establishment of the VUTs, and in Italy, where 50 per cent of early retirement payments are made by employers, that such objectives have been fully attained.

Thus we might conclude by suggesting that the trends noted above have transformed the notion of 'older workers' and their relationship to the labour market. They are no longer people nearing retirement age but, increasingly, they are being defined as unemployable in the labour market or incapable of work.

The social and economic consequences

The Observatory report (Guillemard 1993) highlights three consequences for the fall in labour market activity for men over 55. These are:

1 the consequences for employment and unemployment;
2 the consequences for social protection;
3 the consequences for older people in terms of social integration and their social rights.

Considering the first of these, there was a twofold aim behind the introduction of institutional arrangements to encourage early exit: to reduce unemployment and/or to improve the employment situation. The effects on improving the employment situation were transitory, with little impact upon unemployment levels and therefore difficult to evaluate fully. The manner in which similar arrangements have been abandoned (e.g. in the UK and Germany in 1988 and France in 1986) or had restrictions placed upon them (e.g. Belgium with FNE, the teachers' early retirement pay) throughout the EU reflects upon the mediocrity of the results and the increasing costs of funding them.

Moving to the second observation, the substitution of invalidity and unemployment insurance has altered the fundamental purpose for these social transfers and created a crisis in the legitimacy of social protection systems. For example, in the case of unemployment insurance, rather than being in place to allow labour market flexibility and offer some compensation to (older) workers while unemployed for short periods, they became forms of long-term compensation (often five years or more) for workers who had little chance of obtaining work, thus in effect turning it to a form of pre-retirement pension fund. Additionally, and particularly in the UK, Germany and the Netherlands, there has been a blurring of the boundaries between unemployment and invalidity. As mentioned above, more recently in the UK specific changes have been made in an attempt to redefine these boundaries with the introduction of the job seeker's allowance and incapacity benefit.

With regard to the social status and social rights of older people, it is clear from the Observatory reports that early retirement payments are very popular. This is particularly the case with schemes such as the early retirement solidarity contract in France, the Early Retirement Pay in Denmark and the VUT in the

Netherlands, which allow high replacement incomes. However, there are three main negative consequences of the process of early exit. The movement away from receipt of a retirement pension, often at a predetermined and specific age, towards forms of early exit achieved through a variety of mechanisms has led to a loss of control over the retirement process for the individual and to some degree the power to anticipate it. More often today within the EU countries, it is the employer who may determine when retirement may begin. There has thus been an erosion of the older worker's right to work.

Secondly, entitlement to social rights is now no longer automatic or systematic. The very nature of the contributory principle has been undermined. Previously people may have rested in the knowledge that they would have automatic entitlement to a full pension so long as they had contributed for a specified time and attained a specified age. The flexibility of various methods for early exit, and in particular the use of unemployment and incapacity, may not ensure that a person receives a retirement pension upon retirement. Added to this, the process of early exit has resulted in many older workers who have ceased economic activity preferring to call themselves 'discouraged workers' rather than considering themselves retired (Guillemard 1993).

Finally, the processes described above have resulted in the devaluation and marginalization of the older workers remaining in the labour market. For example, evidence from the Observatory indicates that those over 50 years are over-represented in the long-term unemployed in most countries of the Union and those over 45 experience age discrimination in terms of promotion recruitment and training (see later in this chapter). We will consider these trends by looking in more detail at the situation of older workers in the UK.

The UK case

In the UK, as in most industrial countries, there has been a long-term decline in the participation of older people in the labour force and the active encouragement of early exit, especially during the late 1970s and early 1980s. Among older men, economic activity has declined steadily over the course of this century. At the turn of the century more than two-thirds of men aged 65 and over were in the labour force. By 1951 this proportion had halved and by 1989 it had fallen to only nine per cent. Moreover, as Table 5.2 shows, since the mid-1970s the decline in labour force participation among older men has spread into the age groups below pension age. This contrasts with the situation of older women (55–9) whose participation in the labour force has tended to increase slightly since the 1950s. This is primarily due to increased activity among married women aged 55–9, because activity rates have declined among non-married women in this age group and all women in older age groups (Table 5.2). The decline in the workforce participation of older people, as previously noted, is a pan-European phenomenon, but the main falls in participation took place a few years later in the UK than in comparable EU countries. Moreover, the levels of economic activity are higher in the UK than in the EU as a whole, and this is particularly the case for women aged 50–9.

Table 5.2   Economic activity rates of older women and men in Britain, 1951–94

Age	1951	1961	1971	1975	1981	1985	1990	1994
Women								
55–9	29.1	39.2	50.9	52.4	53.4	52.2	55.0	55.7
60–4	14.1	19.7	28.8	28.6	23.3	18.9	22.7	25.6
65+	4.1	4.6	6.3	4.9	3.7	3.0	3.4	3.2
Men								
55–9	95.0	97.1	95.3	93.0	89.4	82.6	81.5	76.1
60–4	87.7	91.0	86.6	82.3	69.3	55.4	54.4	51.2
65+	31.1	25.0	23.5	19.2	10.3	8.5	8.7	7.5

Source: Taylor and Walker (1995), Table 1, p. 142.

Unemployment rates among both older men and older women in the UK are lower than those of younger people. However, such statistics are misleading because they exclude large numbers of older people who are discouraged from seeking employment but who are, in effect, in a condition of long-term unemployment or non-employment (Walker 1985a; Casey and Laczko 1989). Many have more recently been 'signed off' the unemployment register and claimed invalidity benefit rather than unemployment benefit. This shift in substantial numbers of people off the register by this means was one of the reasons for the introduction of the new incapacity benefit. This has more stringent eligibility criteria, relating to ill-health or incapacity to work, than the invalidity benefit it replaced.

However, the rapid decline in the workforce participation of older men in the late 1970s was closely associated with the rapid rise in unemployment. Precise dividing lines between unemployment, early retirement and disability have always been difficult to draw but in recession this problem is particularly acute among older workers, who may prefer the description 'early retired', even though they may have been receiving unemployment or invalidity benefit rather than a pension.

When they are unemployed, older workers (i.e. those aged over 50) are more likely than younger groups to be long-term unemployed (one year or more). For example, in January 1992 in the UK, 39 per cent of older workers compared with 29 per cent of those aged 25–49 and 12 per cent of those aged 18–24 were unemployed for over a year. They are also more likely to be unemployed for very long periods. For example, 19 per cent of older workers compared with eight per cent of those aged 25–49 and 12 per cent of those aged 18–24 were unemployed for three years or more. The figures for those unemployed for five or more years were 13 per cent, five per cent and less than one per cent respectively.

Figures for July 1995 indicate a hardening of these trends. Thus among men aged over 50, some 48.5 per cent were unemployed for over a year as against nearly 45 per cent of men aged 25–49. For those unemployed in excess of two years, nearly 33 per cent were aged over 50 compared with 28 per cent aged 25–49 and ten per cent who were aged below 25 (Table 5.3). However, these

Table 5.3 Duration of unemployment by age, 13 July 1995, in the UK (percentages)

Duration of unemployment in weeks	Age groups						
	<25	*25–39*	*40–9*	*50–4*	*55–9*	*60+*	*All*
Men							
Up to 13	37.4	23.2	21.0	19.8	16.4	29.7	25.9
13–26	16.7	14.7	14.3	15.5	12.7	22.3	15.2
26–52	20.5	18.5	17.0	20.4	15.3	29.4	18.6
52–104	15.2	17.3	15.9	16.1	16.7	9.8	16.3
104 and over	10.1	26.3	31.9	31.1	38.8	8.7	24.0
Total	100	100	100	100	100	100	100
Number	455,736	740,654	293,712	128,399	117,474	22,655	1,758,630
Women							
Up to 13	47.9	34.0	31.1	26.0	19.7	14.4	37.1
13–26	15.8	18.0	17.9	17.5	14.3	14.9	16.9
26–52	18.6	21.3	18.8	19.0	17.2	18.3	19.4
52–104	12.0	13.7	14.5	15.3	16.8	12.6	13.5
104 and over	5.6	13.0	17.6	22.1	31.9	39.8	13.0
Total	100	100	100	100	100	100	100
Number	216,300	184,261	93,427	44,500	38,724	334	577,546

Source: Department of Employment, *Employment Gazette*, September 1995, p. S25.

figures are based upon the unemployment (benefit-based) count and, as we noted above, they do not contain large numbers of older people who may have been claiming invalidity benefit or incapacity benefit. Among women over 55 there are much higher percentages of them experiencing very long-term unemployment (i.e. over two years) than among younger women: up to three times the average.

Older employees are also more prone to be made redundant than younger ones – which is partly a function of the industrial sectors that they have been concentrated in, especially manufacturing, and partly because of the age criteria built into the redundancy payments scheme. Thus nearly two-thirds of the non-employed aged 55–9 and two-fifths of those aged 60–4 in the UK left their last employment because of redundancy (including a temporary job coming to an end or early retirement as part of a compulsory redundancy programme) or dismissal. Among the unemployed and discouraged it was three in every four (Casey and Laczko 1989). The rise in unemployment during the early 1980s and again in the early 1990s has affected older people in another way. As noted earlier, older workers have been particularly prone to unemployment and, once unemployed, are less likely than younger people to regain secure employment (Table 5.3). This means that the living standards of many people have been depressed *before* retirement.

Measures aimed at removing older people from the labour market, such as the Job Release Scheme and the removal of the employment availability test for men aged 60–4, reflected the long-term official priority given to tackling youth unemployment. The Job Release Scheme was designed to facilitate the early exit of older workers and their substitution by younger people and, at its peak in the height of the early 1980s recession, some 90,000 older people were receiving allowances. During this period older people were discouraged from seeking work by official agencies and experienced considerable discrimination from employers. In addition both employer organizations and trade unions advocated early retirement as a solution to the problem of unemployment (Walker 1982, 1985b).

With the rapid expansion of the UK economy in the late 1980s this policy was reversed and government ministers began calling on employers to recruit more older people. Measures were introduced to promote an increase in the employment of older people. For example, the Job Release Scheme was scrapped and replaced by the 50 Plus Job-Start Allowance Scheme. This was intended to get older unemployed people into part-time work with the goal of this being translated into full-time employment. An older person received £20 on top of the amount paid by the employer, for up to six months. However, the scheme was too small to affect the longer-term decline in workforce participation of older people and the resistance of employers to taking them on. In all, only 118 people applied for the allowance and the scheme was abandoned in February 1991. There were also changes to regulations concerning the registration for state benefits, so that people over 50 were required to register every two weeks instead of every three months. Restrictions on the amount an older person could earn if working beyond the state retirement age before the state pension was reduced have also been removed.

Meanwhile, in the labour market itself many older workers have reported experiencing age discrimination in job recruitment, training and promotion. In the late 1980s there was evidence that some employers were responding to the contraction in the supply of young entrants to the labour market by encouraging older people to remain in or re-enter the workforce. However, recent research shows that, despite this change of attitude on the part of some employers, older people continue to face considerable discrimination in the labour market. A survey of advertisements placed in Job Centres showed that 11 per cent of vacancies were not open to people aged 60 years or over (Jones and Longstone 1990). A survey undertaken by the Institute of Personnel Management (IPM), in 1987, of advertisements in its own publication found that 32 per cent were age limited. Despite the publication by the IPM of a professional code, two years later it was found that 24 per cent of posts in the IPM's journal still specified age limits (Tillsley 1990).

Other reasons often stated by older people as contributory factors to their being refused jobs are the age of the person doing the interview, that employers are not willing to train older people and that employers have concerns that older people might not be physically fit to do a job. Many older people feel that the only jobs open to them are poorly paid and part time (Taylor and Walker 1991, 1995).

The problem of age discrimination cannot be dismissed as being merely the result of overly pessimistic attitudes on the part of older workers. In fact, older workers appear to have realistic perceptions of their re-employment prospects. For example, a study of redundancy in the Sheffield steel industry found that age was an important determinant of unemployment across all socio-economic groups. For instance, among the skilled-manual group the average number of months spent unemployed, in a three-year period following redundancy, was three times greater for those aged 60–4 than for the under-40s (Westergaard *et al.* 1989).

The conclusion that age discrimination by employers is widespread is supported by other recent research. While a survey of employers found that some were taking more active steps to recruit older people, they were considering older people as being eligible mainly for employment in low-skill, low-responsibility and repetitive jobs. Employers also considered older workers less trainable and, as was shown above, older people tend to receive less training than younger adults. Methods aimed at recruiting more older workers included creating more part-time jobs and giving all part-timers permanent status and pension rights in order to make these jobs more attractive (Metcalf and Thompson 1990). However, this policy militates against those older workers who require full-time employment and the income this provides.

Other recent research has indicated the gradual emergence of more positive attitudes towards older workers on the part of employers. For example, in a national survey of employers with 500 or more employees, 63 per cent agreed that older people are very productive employees and 74 per cent that they are more reliable than younger workers (Taylor and Walker 1992).

Thus, current research suggests that while there are some limited signs of better prospects for some older workers, it is more likely to be the case that they are still being treated as a reserve pool of labour, kept on the periphery of some organizations and the labour market, in low-paid and low-skill jobs with little job security, and are being used as a direct substitution for the dwindling numbers of school leavers.

Despite the change in government policy outlined above, the evidence is that the process of discouraging older workers from seeking employment begins before they even encounter a discriminatory employer. Older people are often told that they are unlikely to find employment because of their age by staff of official job recruitment and placement agencies, such as Job Centres, and therefore they cease looking for work. In addition, people who attend 'restart interviews', which are compulsory for anyone who has been unemployed for over six months, are often told that, because of their age, the prospects of them regaining employment are remote and, therefore, they are advised to discontinue looking for work (Taylor and Walker 1991).

Older workers wanting to retrain also face discrimination. The official Employment Training Scheme for unemployed adults has an age restriction of 63 years. First priority is given to people aged 18–24 who have been unemployed for between six and 12 months; and next, to those people aged 18–50 and unemployed for more than two years. The lowest priority for training is given to those people aged over 50, even though the evidence is that older people both in and out of work already have had less education and training than younger people. Moreover, the employment training budget has recently suffered substantial cutbacks and this is likely further to erode the already poor prospects for training among older people.

The obvious clash between high-level policy pronouncements and discriminatory action at the operational level led in 1991 to the initiative to encourage the Job Centres to ask employers to examine age restrictions on the advertisements they place in Job Centres to see if they are absolutely necessary. Job Centre staff have also now been instructed to refer the most suitable candidate to employers irrespective of age. In 1992, the government announced the establishment of an advisory group on the employment of older workers, which is intended primarily to encourage employers to recognize the advantages of employing this group. But there are no signs, as yet, of changes in attitude on the part of officials themselves or the removal of age barriers on government training schemes, although the age limits for recruitment into the home civil service have been scrapped.

The issue of age discrimination represents a major policy lacuna. Despite evidence of age discrimination, older workers receive no special protection or rights under UK law. For example, employers may sack an individual on grounds of age without being in breach of contract. Older people lose the right to protection against unfair dismissal if they are above the 'upper age limit' – which may be 65 or whatever the 'normal retiring age' happens to be for the job the individual holds. As regards redundancy, it is not permissible for an employer to discriminate on the grounds of race, sex or trade union activities; however, industrial tribunal case law has confirmed that it is acceptable for employers to select workers near retirement age in preference to younger employees (Laczko and Phillipson 1991).

There are only a few countries in the world which have legislated against discrimination – the United States, France, Spain, Canada, Australia and New Zealand – and Ireland may soon join them. Also, in a number of European countries, the right to work is enshrined within a written constitution and labour law has provided all workers with some protection against mandatory exclusion (Whiting *et al.* 1995). The UK government, however, has not legislated against age discrimination and, moreover, has indicated that it would be unwilling to do so. A Department of Employment memorandum, in 1988, stated that it would be neither practical nor beneficial to introduce such legislation in the UK and that: 'Employers should be free to recruit the most suitable workers and not be restricted from doing so by legislation and regulation.' This attitude has recently been endorsed by Anne Widdecombe, the minister then responsible, when she told Parliament that after looking at about 20 countries where legislation against age discrimination had been implemented, she had concluded that it did not work. She further suggested that she would prefer to persuade employers rather than 'cluttering up the statute book for the sake of it' (Widdecombe 1995). However, a survey of major British employers has revealed that a majority actually favour legislation to combat age discrimination (53 per cent in favour, 37 per cent against) (Taylor and Walker 1992).

The grounds on which it is argued that such legislation would not be beneficial – the freedom of employers to employ the most suitable workers without restrictions – appears to deny the evidence that many potentially suitable candidates are not employed simply because of their age. Moreover, legislation would not necessarily restrict the rights of employers to employ the most suitable workers but, rather, would ensure that to deny an individual access to employment because of age would be unlawful, in the same way that existing UK legislation makes unlawful discrimination on grounds of race or sex. In view of the absence of a concerted policy in the field of age discrimination, legislation may have an important symbolic role to play in helping to set the policy agenda and in highlighting unhelpful stereotypes in the labour market (Taylor and Walker 1995).

The House of Commons Employment Committee has made several useful recommendations which stop short of legislation against age discrimination, although most have not been acted upon. First of all, the Committee recommended that the government should make a biannual report on the progress which has been made towards achieving the objective of a 'decade of retirement'. The proposal for a 'decade of retirement' is intended, in part, to combat ageism by abolishing mandatory retirement before the age of 70 and allowing older people greater flexibility in the choice of their retirement (Schuller and Walker 1990). Secondly, the government should mount a campaign with employer organizations, to encourage awareness among employers of the potential worth to them of employing older workers and to challenge ageism on practical grounds. Thirdly, the government should review its own practices on retirement and pensions with the object of allowing its older employees greater choice over their age of retirement. Fourthly, in terms of provision for training, it should be made possible for special attention to be given to the needs of the over-50s, and any unemployed person over 50 should be entitled to a training place. Finally, a pilot scheme should be instituted whereby unemployed people over the age of 55 are given £500 to be used for educational or training purposes. The Committee also recommended that employers submitting advertisements to Job Centres should be challenged if they seek to impose age restrictions, and this measure has been implemented (although a private member's bill, proposed by David Winnick, designed to outlaw age discrimination in job advertisements was opposed by the government and 'talked out' of Parliament on 9 February 1996.)

An omission from these recommendations concerns the definition of unemployment. In the UK it is known that many people, for example older women who gave up paid employment to look after a family but who now wish to return, are not classified as unemployed and so would not be eligible to go on official training schemes. This also applies to other schemes offered by the Department for Education and Employment. A better eligibility criterion might be *any* non-working person. Another omission concerns eligibility for other government schemes, such as the Enterprise Allowance Scheme, where eligibility is restricted to those aged 65 or less.

In addition, the IPM has produced an equal opportunities code which makes several recommendations. First, age should not be used as a primary discriminator in recruitment, selection, promotion and training decisions, and, where age bars are used, the questions should be asked are they necessary and why? Secondly, organizations should consider incorporating in their equal opportunity statements their commitment not to discriminate on the grounds of age. Finally, employers should recognize that older workers can still acquire and retain new knowledge and skills, and should do more to provide counselling in career development and to encourage self-development for all employees. Unfortunately this code has only the limited status of guidance. However, if it was operating in the context of anti-discrimination legislation and a concerted campaign on the part of government, its influence could be substantial. In 1993, the government's 'Getting On' campaign was launched to try to educate employers as to the benefits of recruiting, training and retaining older people. In March 1994, a booklet was sent to 165,000 employers advising them of ways to avoid discriminating against older people and gave examples of good practice from some major UK employers (Taylor and Walker 1995). It remains to be seen whether or not this educative approach will bear fruit.

At the plant level, a number of individual employers have begun to take steps to recruit older workers. These include high-profile recruitment drives by four of the UK's largest retailers: B&Q (a DIY chain), W.H. Smith (bookseller and stationer chain), Sainsbury's and Tesco (supermarket chains). For example, Tesco has had a mature entrance programme since 1988 and B&Q has opened a major store staffed only by older people. Indeed, it has recently been reported that Tesco's oldest employee is 80 and B&Q's 82 (Income Data Services 1996). The management of B&Q have also reported considerable benefits in the use of older workers, including reduced turnover and pilferage and higher levels of customer satisfaction. They recently commissioned a survey among their older workers to consider what effect their employment with them was having. Apart from reporting the beneficial financial and social effects of paid employment with the company, nearly four-fifths of them indicated that they had had experience of age discrimination. Indeed, a quarter of them indicated that they had 'come across it often' when looking for work. Age discrimination was said to be as common among those between 50 and 60 as it was for those over 60, and more common against men than women (Wells and Mosley 1995).

An evaluation of Tesco's programme by the World Health Organization (WHO) found many positive features for older employees, such as exercise, companionship, challenge, stimulation, increased confidence, sense of purpose, happiness, friendship and increased income. There were also advantages in employing older people reported by management: reliability, loyalty, improved customer service, reduced staff turnover, steadying influences on young staff, experience and judgement (Kern 1990). Although initiatives such as these are largely confined to lower-paid employment in the service sector, they do demonstrate that it is possible to change long entrenched recruitment practices and to the benefit of both enterprises and older workers. Moreover, they indicate the potential of a policy aimed at trying to facilitate ageing workers to be more productive.

Now, with the rising cost of pensions and, in some countries, predicted shortages of young entrants to the labour market, attention is being turned towards the potential for postponing retirement. Given the long history of their use as a labour reserve in the UK, older workers themselves may be forgiven if they are a little sceptical about these ebbs and flows in public policy. We have focused upon UK policy here but similar policy trends can be discerned in the other countries of the EU. Looking at the EU as a whole, the

Observatory highlighted these major trends in the relationship between older workers and the labour market:

- falling economic activity after the age of 55, in the context of a longer-term reduction in such activity in later life;
- the removal of public pension systems from their central role as the regulators of exit from the labour market;
- the development of new institutional mechanisms governing exit from the labour market in an unplanned and improvised way;
- the changing definition of the 'older worker' from proximity to pension age to labour market criteria such as employability;
- the adverse social and economic consequences of early exit from the labour force, including its limited impact on unemployment levels, the crisis in legitimacy of social protection systems and the marginalization of older workers;
- the development of new approaches to older workers by some employers and the state, including retention and recruitment policies aimed at older workers and a scaling-down of early-exit measures.

Older women and employment

Earlier we noted that there has been a trend, particularly since the 1950s, towards increasing numbers of older women (55–9) in the UK labour force. This trend has also been noted in Denmark, Germany and Italy at least since 1970. In all three countries the participation rates of men in this age range has been declining over this period. In contrast, the participation rates for both men and women over 65 has declined throughout the EU since 1970.

For the EU as a whole, just over a third of the female population in the 55–9 age group are employed. There are considerable differences between states. Denmark stands out in this respect, with nearly two-thirds of women in this age group in employment. This can be attributed largely to the higher pension age in Denmark together with the social support available for the care of their children (Platz and Petersen 1992). Belgium and Luxembourg have the lowest rates, with 15 and 18 per cent of women in this age group in employment, respectively. After 60 the employment rates drop dramatically and, for the EU as a whole, an average of 14 per cent of women aged 60–4 and just over two per cent for those over 65 are employed. This compares with male labour force participation rates of 72 per cent for those aged 55–9, 37 per cent of those 60–4 and 6.7 per cent of those over 65.

Work or retirement?

In the Eurobarometer survey of people aged 60 and over, some seven out of ten were retired and not working, only six per cent were still employed and the same proportion were retired but still working. The remaining one-fifth either had never held a paid job or had not done so for many years.

The retired were asked if, at the time of their retirement, they would have preferred to stay in employment either full time or part time. The majority (58

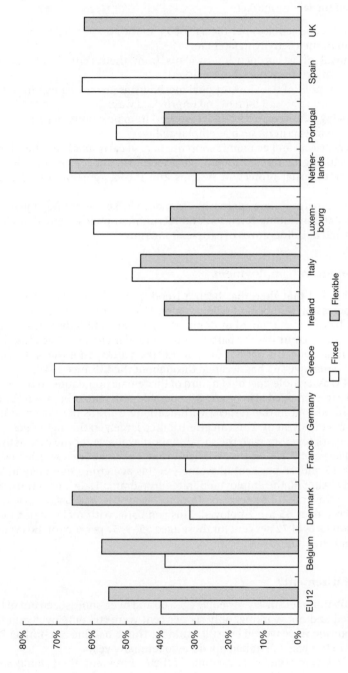

Figure 5.1 Percentages in the general survey favouring flexible or fixed age of retirement.

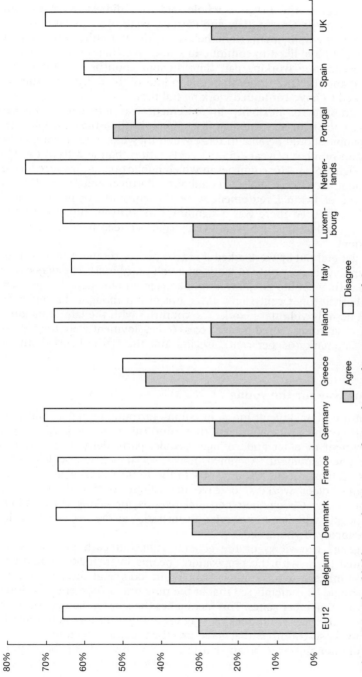

Figure 5.2 Should older people give up work to make way for younger people?

per cent) across the EU as a whole said they did *not* want to continue working. Only in Greece, Italy and Portugal were there majorities in favour of continued employment. Nonetheless, nearly two-fifths of the retired said they would have liked to continue in work. Over half of them would have liked to continue working part time. In four countries – Greece, Ireland, Portugal and the UK – more than one in four of the retired said they would have liked to have continued working full time.

The question of flexibility in retirement was pursued in the general Eurobarometer survey. The majority opinion in the EU as a whole was that older people should be able to retire when they like, after having worked a minimum number of years (55 per cent) rather than at a fixed age (40 per cent) (Figure 5.1). The countries in which public opinion favoured fixed-age retirement are Greece, Italy, Luxembourg, Portugal and Spain. Those most in favour of flexible retirement were the currently employed, but even among the retired there was a significant majority in support. Those who had never held a paid job were evenly split between fixed-age and flexible retirement.

The general public were asked if retired people should be allowed to take paid employment or only to work on a voluntary basis. The majority either said that they should be allowed to take paid employment (43 per cent) or to do both (16 per cent); only three out of ten thought that older people should do only voluntary work. The countries with the largest majorities in favour of granting retired people access to employment were the UK (76 per cent), Denmark (63 per cent), Ireland and the Netherlands (both 50 per cent).

Making way for the young

One of the most difficult moral questions surrounding public policy in this field in recent years has been that concerning the respective rights to employment of older and younger people, particularly at a time of high youth unemployment. As noted above, social policies, such as the Job Release Scheme in the UK and VUT in the Netherlands, have been used to encourage older workers to leave the labour force and make way for younger ones. Giving their personal reasons for taking early retirement, older people will sometimes refer altruistically to the need to provide jobs for unemployed youngsters.

To gauge the views of the general public in each member state we presented them with the proposition, 'people in their 50s should give up work to make way for younger people'. In looking at the results in Figure 5.2 it should be remembered that at the time unemployment was rising in a majority of member states. This fact makes the substantial opposition to the notion of one age group making way for another all the more remarkable. Even in those countries that have practised labour age-group substitution there did not appear to be any enthusiasm for this sort of policy. Moreover, there was hardly any difference in opinion on this question between younger people and older ones. For example, 61 per cent of those aged 15–24 disagreed compared with 66 per cent of those aged 55 and over.

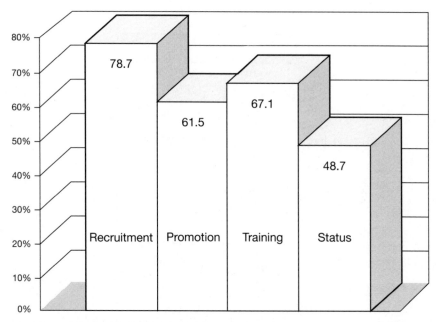

Figure 5.3   Proportion believing older workers are discriminated against in employment for EU12.

Age discrimination

Objective evidence about discrimination on grounds of age is hard to come by, for obvious reasons, and a large-scale public opinion survey such as Eurobarometer is not a sensitive enough vehicle on which to try to collect such information. But this important issue, in personal and policy terms, could not be ignored. The solution was to ask some specific questions concerning job recruitment, promotion, training and the status or position an older worker occupies in his or her organization. By asking these questions of the general public we are avoiding the possible criticism that older workers themselves may be biased in their opinions and may use age discrimination as an excuse for poor performance.

Figure 5.3 shows that an extraordinarily high proportion of citizens in EU countries believed that older workers *are* discriminated against with regard to job recruitment. Indeed, half of the 12 countries sampled had responses of over 80 per cent to this question. Furthermore, significant majorities also believed that such discrimination exists with regard to job promotion and training. In the UK, for example, where as we noted no such legislation exists, over 82 per cent of the sample agreed that older people are discriminated against in recruitment and 77 per cent of them agreed that discrimination occurs in both promotion and training. Critics might justifiably argue that these results often reflect subjective opinion rather than presenting objective facts. Yet, since such a wide cross-section of the 12 member states sampled thought that age discrimination in employment is widespread, it is difficult to argue that it does

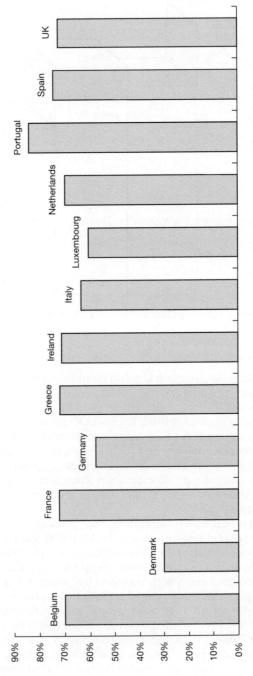

Figure 5.4 Proportion of general public who think their government should introduce laws to stop age discrimination.

not exist. The only item on which there was not, quite, a majority concerned the status or position an older person occupies in an organization, a not altogether surprising finding given the existence of age-related promotion and career patterns.

Equally noteworthy is the fact that there were hardly any differences between age groups in their strong belief that age discrimination exists with regard to employment. Across the age range a significant majority (over 72 per cent) felt it exists, and for those over 25 and under 65, over 81 per cent agreed with the statement. The same uniform response by younger and older workers was found with regard to promotion, training and occupational status. Also, there were no differences between men and women in their responses to these questions.

The final stage of this analysis of issues concerning older workers focuses on government action. There is a great deal of controversy in Europe surrounding the issue of legislation against age discrimination, with some groups representing older workers arguing that it is essential to protect this group in the face of widespread discrimination and some policy makers responding that it would be unenforceable. What does the general public think? By a majority of two to one they favour such government action (in fact less than one in five said that the state should *not* introduce such legislation, so if those who did not express an opinion are excluded the majority would be four to one) (Figure 5.4).

6

Health and social care

It has been noted that older people in Europe are now living longer, healthier and more productive lives than ever before. It was suggested that this increasing longevity is a sign of social and economic progress, especially the successful intervention in death and disease by public health measures. However, this demographic shift towards an ageing European community will inevitably result in more and more people who are likely to need some personal care or support in later life, because of the close association between disability and advanced old age. It is important not to get this out of proportion: the majority of older people, even in the fourth age, are able to look after themselves adequately or with only minimal assistance from others. For example, 90 per cent of older Swedes live in their own home, five per cent with their children and only the remaining five per cent in institutions.

Moreover, in the majority of EU countries, the state plays a relatively minor role in the care of older people either as direct providers or funders. If help is required, it usually comes first from the family, but the demand for informal and formal care is rising. Thus an increase in the proportion of older people requiring care has important implications for both families (and women in particular) as well as governments. Therefore, yet again, this was an issue that had to be addressed in the Eurobarometer surveys. However, before reporting some of the interesting results from these surveys, we provide a background overview of the state of health and social services in the Union, which is based upon the reports written for the European Observatory.

Health and social care services

We begin with a word of caution. Much of the information about the provision of health and social services remains piecemeal, and cross-national comparisons are difficult to make. It is extremely difficult to compare very divergent systems based upon different political and social structures. More cross-national and comparative research is needed, as well as more indicative and comparative statistical information around the issues facing older people and health care. Having made this qualification, the main policy issues highlighted by the Observatory were:

- While the majority of older people are in fairly good health, this group is responsible for a greater than average use of health services.
- The high institutional and organizational fragmentation of health and social services frequently entails serious problems of coordination.
- There is a general consensus that community care is the most appropriate policy for the care of older people.
- Marked variations in the supply of both residential and domiciliary services between member states.
- In a number of countries there is severe under-supply of community care services.
- Recent policy developments include: the containment of growth of health expenditure; the definition of policy priorities in the care of older people; the provision of adequate coverage for long-term care; the reorganization of residential care; and the introduction of new incentives for the development of community care.

In most countries of the EU the provision of medical and social services for older people is distinguished by its complexity. This complexity requires that, for the purposes of the discussion, we must distinguish between medical and social services and between domiciliary care and residential care. Within medical services there is a further division between acute and long-term care for treatment (associated particularly with disabled older people). Added to this complexity, a further key issue facing most of the Union's health and social services provision is the multiplicity of providers, who are regulated by different legislation and are financed by a variety of agencies. Thus there are serious issues of coordination between services.

The majority of the 12 member states considered by the Observatory, have some form of national health service. The exceptions, Belgium, France, Germany and Luxembourg, have health systems which are based upon sickness insurance, which tend to be funded from contributions rather than general taxation. The Netherlands has a system which combines a compulsory sickness insurance scheme limited to low-income earners and pensioners, with a universal scheme for exceptional medical expenses, for example long-term care. However, in those countries which have a predominantly insurance-based system there is considerable variation. In Belgium and France the scheme covers both acute and long-term care, whereas in Germany long-term domiciliary care is covered, but long-term care in nursing homes is a private risk. It should be noted that in Germany a public insurance scheme for long-term care has been introduced recently.

All countries in the EU aim to keep older people within their own community or social environments for as long as possible – a policy of community care or ageing in place. Yet, having said this, the number of places in residential care has expanded over the past 20 years, a trend which has halted only recently or in some cases been reversed, for example in Greece. The funding of such care varies considerably between countries. Both Denmark and the Netherlands have publicly funded schemes, with the former being funded through general taxation and the latter through the medical insurance scheme. However, some residential homes for older people in Netherlands have their costs borne by the private assets of their residents. Those unable to afford to make such payments have up to 80 per cent of their pension paid towards the cost, the remainder coming from the social security budget.

In Ireland, Portugal and Spain, outside the private sector, residential care is publicly financed, with a large contribution being made from the pensions of the residents. In Germany and Luxembourg the insurance scheme covers only medical expenses, so that long-term care must be borne from private resources, with some means-tested assistance, though in the German case the care insurance system will be fully operational by 2000. Italy and the UK are the only countries with a large number of private residential and nursing homes.

Although there is some variation in how incapacity is measured among European countries it is still valid to claim that severe incapacity affects only a small minority of older people. For example, evidence from the European Observatory on Ageing and Older People suggested that the proportion of people over 65 who are severely incapacitated is below ten per cent and is less than five per cent for the population aged 60–9. However, as might be expected, this figure increases to 30 per cent for those over the age of 80. Although there is considerable variation among countries, the most prominent illnesses among older people would appear to be cardiovascular diseases, with various forms of dementia listed as being a particular challenge for those in the fourth age.

The higher rates of morbidity among this older group has resulted in higher expenditure on health services. Observatory reports indicate that this is usually two to three times higher than their proportion in the population. For example, in 1993, although the older population in Denmark accounted for 15 per cent of the population, they accounted for 49 per cent of the hospital bed days. Similarly in Germany, pensioners accounted for 29 per cent of all sickness insurance members but 52 per cent of all hospital expenditure, and in the Netherlands although they comprised 13 per cent of the population at the time, of those aged over 65, 25 per cent are hospital patients. Similar trends were noted in the majority of the 12 countries of the EU.

Yet many countries have reported that geriatric medicine (now more commonly referred to as health care for older people) has only recently been recognized as a specialism, for instance in Denmark, France, Germany, the Netherlands and Spain, with only the UK and Italy having a long-established medical specialism in this field. When they do attend hospitals as inpatients older people tend to stay longer than the average. This is more often not related to a preponderance of serious illness but more to do with a mis-allocation of acute bed space or with the lack of family support at home and insufficient access to specialist long-term care facilities.

Ireland and the Netherlands can be regarded as notable exceptions to these trends. In both these countries there are highly developed mechanisms which reduce lengthy waiting lists and excessive length of stay in nursing homes.

Similarly, in Belgium and France a policy has been developed to shift older people from acute care to the care sector. Although the principal motivation for this appears to involve lowering the cost of sickness insurance, it may have negative consequences for the older people concerned in terms of the level and nature of their care.

Yet long-term care tends to be predominantly a family-oriented task. Most of the responsibility for this care tends to be placed disproportionately upon women in private households, the notable exception to this being Denmark. This raises a dilemma for policy makers, since declining birth rates combined with the rise in labour force participation of women and higher incidence of divorce has led to a reduced potential source of care for older people in poor health. A new system of long-term care is urgently required in many countries of the Union, since the predominant forms of care based largely upon filial obligation may soon be impracticable. They could be funded either through a long-term health care insurance scheme (as in Belgium and Germany), based in either the public or private sector, or through increased taxation. We return to this issue later in this chapter since it was one of those raised within the Eurobarometer survey.

Indeed, the Observatory has reported that several countries have begun to draft plans for the future of health care for their senior citizens. For example, Belgium has a round table of health experts dating from 1988 and Denmark has passed legislation on old-age policies in this field since the late 1980s. In France, each department has been obliged since 1982 to develop a gerontological plan and in 1991 the national government introduced a plan covering several years for the future development of health care. Germany similarly passed a Federal plan in 1992 and Ireland issued its plan for older people, 'The Years Ahead', in 1988 at about the same time as Luxembourg developed its 'National Programme for Older People'. This planning has been accompanied by some major implementation. The Dutch government reformed its health and social care legislation very recently and, as mentioned above, Germany has just introduced a system of compulsory long-term health care insurance.

The clear distinction made in most countries between medical services and social services is not reflected in Denmark, Italy and the Netherlands, where the responsibility for nursing care and social services is shared by the same provider or financing agency. For those with national health services, organizational responsibility is clearly divided between medical and social services, with the former under direct control of a central governmental control, usually a minister of health, and the latter to the local authorities. A similar division is reported for those countries with a predominately social insurance system, with a marked distinction being made between the two in Belgium, France, Germany and Luxembourg.

Within the long-term care and home help sectors, provision is supported largely by both for-profit and non-profit private-sector suppliers. Again there are exceptions, Denmark being the only country with a high level of public provision in counties and municipalities. The voluntary non-profit sector is strong in Germany, Belgium and the Netherlands. There is a significant involvement of religious voluntary organizations in the Catholic and Orthodox countries (Greece, Italy, Ireland, Portugal and Spain).

We referred earlier to the serious problems of coordination which affect most of the countries' medical and health service provision and are a feature of most of the Observatory's country reports in this area. With increasing fragmentation and division of responsibility has come increasing discontinuity of service provision. This may often result in ineffective case management within a framework which emphasizes flexible consideration of older people's needs. From the reports it would appear that Denmark and the Netherlands are the two countries where most progress has been made. In Denmark this has been achieved by the merging of home-help services with domiciliary care to overcome the conflict of professional roles between social workers and nurses. In the Netherlands a more flexible case management regime is in operation so as to improve coordination between service sectors, and in Belgium coordination centres are being established at a local level.

The increasing use of community care or 'ageing in place', mentioned earlier, throughout the Union is one of the clearest trends noted in the Observatory reports, although the motivation behind these policy shifts is not always as clear. However, there is still a proportion of the older population who require some form of residential care. Despite wide variation in definition, three main types of residential accommodation can be identified within the Union. The first is sheltered housing, in which people without a need or desire for extended care live in separate apartments but share common services. Secondly, there are residential homes for older people who no longer maintain independent households. It is usually the case that the residents require limited amounts of care, share a room with other persons, have common meals and have access to services such as home helps. The final form is the nursing home for those in need of extended care. Day care centres can provide a 'bridge' between residential and domiciliary care.

The supply of such forms of accommodation for older people shows marked variation among the countries of the Union. However, the note of caution expressed earlier applies when considering these figures in comparative context because of the wide discrepancy in national definitions and in many cases the overlap of the three forms identified. Thus interpretation is difficult in terms of policy evaluation. However, three groupings of countries can be discerned regarding the provision of residential care. The first, with a high level of supply (approaching ten per cent of the population over 65), occurs in the Benelux countries and Denmark. The second, middle group comprises France, Germany and Ireland, where supply is around five per cent. The countries with low levels of supply, forming the third group, include Greece, Italy, Portugal and Spain, where provision is around three per cent. The UK is difficult to place since it has a higher level of sheltered housing than the other countries.

The overwhelming policy priority of community care over residential care has been clearly expressed in the case of Belgium and Denmark, which established official moratoria on residential care. In France, Germany, Ireland, Italy and the Netherlands similar policy shifts can be discerned towards alternatives to residential care. Where there are no explicit policy statements on community care (for example in Greece, Portugal and Spain) the Observatory reports clearly note that governments plan an expansion of community care.

One of the major explanations for such a development can be attributed to fiscal retrenchment. Most governments seem convinced that domiciliary care is a less expensive form of provision. Several of the Observatory reports show that there exists a 'care gap' despite extensions to service provision. There is widely reported evidence of severe under-supply of community services in most countries. Thus the shift in the role of care has been placed upon (more often female) family members. The Observatory reports clearly show that reductions in long-term residential accommodation were not always counter-balanced by an expansion in domiciliary care. For example, in Italy, although 15 per cent of older people need home care, only approximately one per cent receive it. In Denmark it was reported that widening access to care was accompanied by a reduction in the number of hours provided. We explore these issues later in this chapter when we consider the results from the Eurobarometer survey.

Health and social care in the UK

Having provided an outline of the nature of health and social services in Europe our attention turns to consider the position in the UK. In the UK the public sector is by far the largest provider of health and personal social services. Although the numbers of people covered by private medical insurance more than doubled between 1978 and 1987 there were still only 5.3 million people insured on the latter date. As far as the social services are concerned, there has been a rapid expansion in the private residential and nursing home sector during the 1980s, but taking all kinds of formal services – residential, day care and domiciliary – into account, the state remains dominant.

The funding and operation of health and social services is separate. The NHS, which is largely free at the point of use, is funded by central taxation and the Department of Health is responsible for the distribution of resources to regional health authorities and directing overall health policy. The NHS comprises two main sections: hospital and community health services and family (or general) practitioner services. Budgets are cash limited and services are free at the point of use. Acute services take the bulk of health authority expenditure (46 per cent), with specialist medical services for older people comprising 13 per cent. Reforms implemented through the NHS and Community Care Act 1990 have attempted to create an 'internal market' for health care, with a division between 'purchasers' (now mainly the general practitioner fund-holders and district health authorities) and 'providers' of health care (the newly created NHS trusts, private health care suppliers and the voluntary sector).

Community health services include community nurses, health visitors, community psychiatric and mental handicap nurses, therapy services and chiropody. The family practitioner services cover the general medical, dental and ophthalmic services. Recent policy changes have introduced charges for dental examinations and abolished free NHS sight tests (exemptions are available on a means-tested basis) but general practitioner (GP) services remain free of charge.

Medicines prescribed under the NHS remain free to all those over state pension age. Indeed, in 1992, 70 per cent of all prescriptions dispensed were exempt from charge, although this figure also includes contraceptive devices (*Health and Personal Social Services Statistics for England* 1993). Consultation rates with GPs tend to be higher for women than for men with the greatest difference occurring in the 16–44 age group. For example, in 1992, 18 per cent of women in this age range consulted a GP against nine per cent of men (General Household Survey 1994).

The personal social services are funded partly out of central and partly from local taxation. The Department of Health sets general policy guidelines but the services themselves are organized and operated by 116 local authorities in England and Wales, which are headed by elected representatives. While the NHS is underpinned by a uniform system of organization, the personal social services are characterized by diversity. In Scotland social services incorporate the probation service. In Northern Ireland they are integrated with health services and operated by joint area boards. Outside Northern Ireland it is frequently the case that health authority and local authority boundaries are not co-terminous. There are wide variations between local authorities, largely depending on their political colour, in the extent of the services they provide. For example, the proportion of home helps per 1000 people aged 65 and over varies by a factor of four between different authorities.

The personal social services are operated by social services departments (SSDs) in England and Wales and they have responsibility, including statutory responsibility in some cases, for the care of all groups in need, including children. Social services for older people are traditionally organized on a tripartite basis: residential, day care and domiciliary services. The bulk of domiciliary support is provided by the home help or home care service, expenditure on which accounts nationwide for well over a third of the total local authority domiciliary care budget. The service offers help with personal and domestic tasks such as washing, dressing, cleaning, laundry, shopping, preparing meals and managing medication. Other domiciliary services for older people comprise meals on wheels, disability equipment and adaptations to homes, transport, respite care and social work. In addition to these local authority services there is a large voluntary sector, often working under contract to SSDs, providing services such as day care to older people and a substantial private sector of residential care.

As is the case in the rest of the Union, when older people require it the main source of non-specialized care is the family. Yet, the main providers of this informal care within the family are female kin, even though a substantial number of carers nowadays are men. Thus the numbers of very severely disabled people aged 80 or more living in private households is some two-thirds more than the number living in all hospitals, nursing and residential homes put together. Among those aged 70–9 the ratio is three times as many living in their own or relatives' homes as in communal establishments. In a recent random survey of people aged 75 and over in England's fourth largest city, Sheffield, it was found that only nine per cent received any regular help from non-relatives (Qureshi and Walker 1989).

Since 1979 a cost-effectiveness imperative has held sway over health and social services and a concerted effort has been made by central government to increase the role of the private sector on the one hand and reduce the provider role of the public sector on the other. The first main element of this policy was the use of the social security system to subsidize places in private residential and nursing homes. As a result there was a mushrooming of private homes in the early 1980s: a 97 per cent increase in places between 1979 and 1984, and by 1990 the number of places in such homes had risen by 130 per cent since 1979. The first year in which the proportion of all places which were in private homes (44 per cent) was greater than that in local authority homes (43 per cent) was 1988, with voluntary homes accounting for only 13 per cent of all places. Between 1989 and 1990 alone, the proportion of beds in private residential homes for older people rose by nine per cent while beds in private nursing homes increased by 27 per cent. The number of beds in local authority homes declined during the 1980s.

While in the NHS, between 1978 and 1988, the total number of geriatric beds fell by 5000 to 53,000, short-stay admissions to local authority homes increased, signalling their increasing use as respite care. Well over half of older people in private residential homes have all or most of their fees paid by the social security system. The increase in the number of people in residential care and in nursing homes relying on social assistance (income support) to pay their fees was 250 per cent between 1979 and 1984 and 1475 per cent between 1979 and 1990. Not surprisingly the rapid growth in the numbers with public support living in private residential and nursing homes – from 12,000 in 1979 to 220,000 in April 1991 – led to a similarly rapid increase in this element of the social security budget: from £10 million in 1979 to £1872 million in May 1991.

The second main plank in the policy pursued since 1979 has been the promotion of informal and voluntary alternatives to the social services. To aid the development of voluntary help, self-help and informal care, a series of special initiatives, such as the 'Care in the Community' and the 'Helping the Community to Care' programmes, were introduced. As a result, service provision has begun to become more fragmented and diverse than in the previous, consensus era. The role of the state as a direct provider of services has been reduced and measures currently being implemented will reinforce these trends. In particular, it is intended that local authority SSDs should be concerned primarily with funding and managing or 'enabling' care services rather than providing them.

Current policy towards the health and social services is enshrined in the NHS and Community Care Act 1990. This Act was based on two white papers, one, *Working for Patients*, on health and the other, *Caring for People*, on social services (Department of Health 1989a, 1989b). Both white papers reinforced the government's commitments to community care and the encouragement of a range of services to enable older people to live as independently as possible in their own homes. GPs are given a key role in assessing need and health promotion. They are expected to offer a visit to those aged 75 and over to assess home environment, the availability of informal carers and social, physical and mental wellbeing, and, where relevant, to provide advice on or refer individuals to different services.

Considerable emphasis is placed on the concepts of 'consumer choice' and independence. The stated aim is to 'give people a greater say in how they live their lives and the services they need to help them to do so' (Department of

Health 1989a). The majority of the current changes support the local provision of services. Where they have to seek long-stay care, 'people should be able to exercise the maximum possible choice about the home they enter' (Department of Health 1989b). Arrangements made by the SSD should be sufficiently 'flexible' to permit this. It is also intended that service providers make practical support for carers a 'high priority' and it is argued that assessment of care needs 'should always take account of the needs of caring family, friends and neighbours' (Department of Health 1989b).

The main structural changes being made to help to ensure that these policy goals are realized were a new contract for GPs which put a premium on preventive health care and, as far as social services were concerned, a completely new managerial and financial framework. The aim is to transform local authority SSDs from what was regarded as 'monopolistic providers' into 'enabling agencies' concerned primarily with managing and purchasing services. SSDs are responsible for assessing individual need and designing appropriate 'packages of care'. The medium through which these tasks will be achieved is care management. SSDs have a responsibility to secure a 'diversity of provision'. They can still be direct providers but they are expected to make use, wherever possible, of services from voluntary and private providers.

To help achieve these ends, a new funding structure for community care has been implemented. This gives local authorities financial responsibility through a single unified budget, paid by central government through the revenue support grant for local authorities, for the care of older people, whether they are in residential care or living in their own homes. The resources which would otherwise have financed care through social security payments to people in residential and nursing homes were transferred to local authorities, which are responsible for all public funding of care for older people and other groups in need. Additional social security funding will be given to residents in private and voluntary homes, but not those in public-sector homes, so there is an incentive for local authorities to privatize their residential homes. SSDs are being encouraged to introduce competitive tendering and to move towards contractual partnerships with private and voluntary agencies. SSDs will be expected to charge older people for the use of day care and domiciliary services.

Current issues

The main policy issues with regard to the provision of health and social services for older people in the UK arise from the implementation of the major structural changes outlined above (Audit Commission 1992). These mainly effect the social services, but in addition the hospital services are undergoing a radical overhaul following the introduction of an internal market based on competition for patients between independent hospital trusts. This raises obvious fears that 'expensive' older patients will not prove attractive to hospitals involved in such an internal market. In fact a report has suggested that, following the passing of the 1990 Act, up to one-third of health authorities are attempting to abolish all long-stay beds (Age Concern 1991). This was confirmed by a subsequent report from the King's Fund Institute which criticized the NHS for abandoning long-stay geriatric care and, in doing so, effecting the replacement of free NHS care by private care for which older people and their families have to pay part or all of the cost (Henwood 1992). The extent to which the NHS can operate in a more preventive mode is also an issue of great importance with regard to future generations of older people.

The aim of policy with regard to older people is said to be community care, but residential care has been the fastest growing sector by far over the last decade because, for political reasons, a 'perverse incentive' was given to older people on income support to enter private homes. Policy makers face a dilemma with regard to this substantial and growing private sector of residential and nursing homes. In some parts of the UK private-sector beds already outnumber public-sector ones. The outcome for older people is that many have ended up in residential care when they would not have needed to if resources had been available in the community. The government has tried to limit the cost of this policy by not uprating subsidies in line with costs, but this has resulted in large numbers of owners of private residential homes having their homes reclassified as nursing homes in order to attract higher subsidies. Unfortunately it is difficult to see how this policy can be overturned in the present political climate.

A considerable body of evidence has also been built up over more than a decade concerning the abuse of older people in some residential homes (public and private), and a national survey in 1992 (Ogg and Bennett 1992; see also Penhale 1993 and DoH 1992) showed that such abuse exists in private households as well. This abuse may be financial, psychological, physical, sexual or neglect. A growing concern with the widespread nature of elder abuse caused the launch of Action on Elder Abuse in 1993, which was the first such nationally run body attempting to raise awareness of the issue as well as to find effective ways in which to reduce its occurrence. In their literature they have defined abuse as, 'a single or repeated act or lack of appropriate action occurring within any relationship where there is an expectation of trust which causes harm or distrust to an older person.'

Some ten per cent of carers admitted in the survey to abusing the older person they were caring for, while five per cent of older people said they had experienced verbal abuse and two per cent physical abuse or financial abuse. The latter figure implies a total of 500,000 in the population as a whole experiencing physical abuse.

There have been many innovative projects in the social care of older people over the last decade. These include small-scale projects aimed at extending home help tasks in a more flexible way, supporting the carers of older people and working with specific groups of older people such as those from ethnic minorities or those suffering Alzheimer's disease. At the other end of the spectrum there are large-scale innovations that have attracted substantial local and/or national funding. The best-known of these is the Kent Community Care Scheme (Davies and Challis 1986) and its various spin-offs. This project has given prominence to the role of the care manager as the linch pin of care and has had considerable success in demonstrating that it is possible to delay the need for residential or hospital services by the effective organization of packages of care in the community.

In common with other schemes, like the Neighbourhood Services Project in

Dinnington, the Kent project has sought to organize informal or quasi-formal helpers into a support network or to sustain existing networks. In contrast there are a few innovations that have focused on change *within* social services and the development of more flexible forms of service provision. The main example of this genre is the Neighbourhood Support Units initiative in Sheffield. These Units aimed to provide the whole range of services required by older people in their own homes, from routine domiciliary assistance through to comprehensive care equivalent to that available in a residential setting (Walker and Warren 1996).

Important developments in the way SSDs interact with service users, including older people, have resulted from the changes in the organization of community care. As part of the community care planning process, many SSDs engaged in a dialogue with older service users about their needs and the services they required. Leading examples were Birmingham SSD's 'Community Care and You' consultation initiative and Wolverhampton SSD's document 'Old Enough to Live Independently', a synopsis of which was sent to everyone in Wolverhampton over the age of 70.

An innovation that has spread from the UK to some of its European neighbours is the hospice movement, founded in 1967 by Dame Cicely Saunders. This movement aims to curtail some aspects of high-tech (or tertiary) medicine, which has the capacity to delay people's physical death long after their social death and reduce terminally ill patients to helpless objects. The idea therefore is to keep people not only 'alive' but 'in life' for as long as possible. There are now over 200 such hospices in the UK, and some have been established in the urban areas of Ireland. Denmark allows close relatives of dying people to take leave of absence with part of any lost income being reimbursed by the state. Germany, Luxembourg and the Netherlands have reported a recent growth in hospices. In the German case between 1993 and 1995 the number of hospices in Bavaria has increased from seven to 22. The Federal Department for Families and Older People is encouraging the development of the hospice movement by providing guidelines and training of hospice staff (*Ageing International* 1995a). The growth of the movement in Germany has been limited, however, by the nature of the sickness insurance scheme, which does not cover such costs.

Caring for older people in Europe

We now focus our attention upon the results of the Eurobarometer survey. Importantly, the survey considered some of the contentious policy matters mentioned above in an attempt to gauge the attitudes of the citizens of the Union to the issue of care.

In order to establish a bench mark for some questions about the receipt of care among older people, it was necessary to know the incidence of functional incapacity. To do so, the surveys employed a standard question from British social surveys (e.g. GHS) concerning the presence of a longstanding illness, disability or infirmity which limits an individual's activities. This has been shown to be an effective method of distinguishing those suffering from significant disability.

Accordingly, just under two-fifths (38 per cent) of the population aged 60 and over said they were suffering from functional incapacity. However, the variations were quite wide between countries, from 53 per cent in Greece to 22 per cent in Belgium, and this suggests some variation in the interpretation of the question. Predictably there was an association between age and disability: 32 per cent of those aged 60–4 reported a limiting longstanding illness or disability compared with 47 per cent of those aged 80 and over. But, even in this oldest group, the majority did not regard themselves as disabled to any major extent.

Next we asked about the care that older people were receiving (if any). Here the focus was on regular assistance with personal care and household tasks that people need help with because they find them difficult to do by themselves. The results are shown in Figure 6.1. Although it should be recognized that these data exclude those living in institutions, two points should be emphasized. First, relatively small proportions were receiving care, often well below 30 per cent, apart from Greece, Portugal and Luxembourg. Second, these figures cannot be read as a proxy for the *need* for care since it is likely that some people in need are not getting any help. (Disability is a better indicator of the likely need for help and assistance than is care provision.) Again, there were big differences between those in their third and fourth ages with regard to receipt of care: 18 per cent of the 60–4 year-olds compared with 59 per cent of those aged 80 and over.

Who are the main supporters of older people in need of care? Looking at the EU as a whole, adult children were the most frequently mentioned carers (40 per cent), followed by spouses (32 per cent), private paid help (11 per cent), other relatives (14 per cent), the public social services (13 per cent), friends (six per cent), neighbours (six per cent) and voluntary organizations (three per cent). Therefore, as demonstrated by previous research and referred to above, family members are by far the main providers of care: two-thirds of the care being supplied to older people in the special Eurobarometer survey came from within their own families.

Looking at children first, one-half of them were living with the older person and the other half were supplying care from outside of the older person's household. In-house care was most common in Greece (39 per cent), Italy (34 per cent) and Spain (30 per cent) and least common in the Netherlands (two per cent) and Denmark (four per cent). Out-of-house care by adult children was most common in Germany (32 per cent), Belgium (27 per cent) and Greece (26 per cent) and least so in France (12 per cent) and Italy (13 per cent).

The role played by spouses differed considerably between EU countries. In Greece 47 per cent of those receiving care were being helped by a spouse; in Portugal it was 44 per cent and in Germany 40 per cent. At the other end of the scale only eight per cent were assisted by a spouse in the Netherlands and 19 per cent in Denmark. The role of paid private help also differed widely between the member states. Only three countries reported more than one-fifth of assistance being provided by private paid help: France (27 per cent), the Netherlands (33 per cent) and the UK (21 per cent). In comparison Greece, Ireland, Portugal and Spain recorded only three to five per cent of care coming from this source.

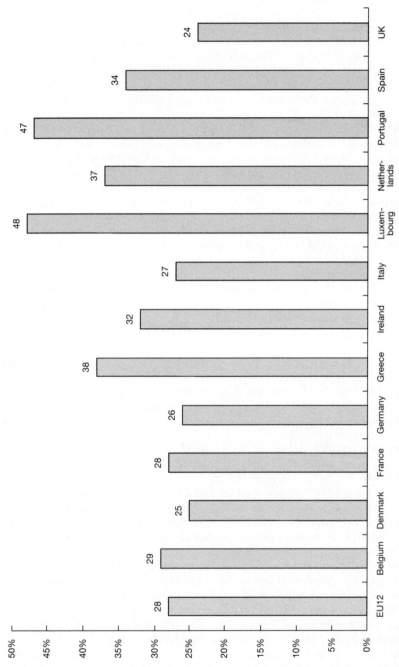

Figure 6.1 Proportion of older people receiving help or assistance with personal care or household tasks.

Table 6.1 Percentage of different age groups receiving regular help or assistance from spouses and the public services

	60–4	65–9	70–4	75–9	80+
Spouse	54	44	33	25	16
Public services	8	8	10	13	20

Not surprisingly, the public social services figured significantly in those countries with the most developed infrastructures of service provision. Of those countries sampled, Denmark has the most extensive system of home care provision and, in this survey, more than two-thirds of those receiving care were being assisted by the social services. Next in line came the Netherlands and the UK, with just over one-quarter receiving such help, followed by Belgium and France with just under one-fifth. After that no other EU country made it into double figures (Ireland was closest at nine per cent).

Looking at these results from the perspective of age, the older the group the less likely it was that care would be provided by a spouse and the greater was the likelihood that it would be provided by the public social services. This, to some extent 'substitution', relationship developed as shown in Table 6.1. The roles of neighbours and the voluntary sector also increased with the age of the person in receipt of care but nowhere near as significantly as that of the public sector. Even so, the public sector clearly did not fully compensate for the loss of spouse care. The role of private paid help remained more or less constant across the age range, as did that of children and other relatives. Therefore these data suggest that there is something of a *care gap* left by the loss of spouses (Walker 1985b; Qureshi and Walker 1989). Given the disproportionate share of care for older people borne by women it is important to note that they were far less likely than men to receive assistance from a spouse: 18 per cent compared with 53 per cent of men.

Are families willing to care?

Despite data, such as those presented in the previous section, showing the crucial role of the family in the care of older people, the myth has been perpetuated that families are now less willing to care for their relatives than they were in past times. This myth has been debunked countless times by both historical and contemporary research (Laslett 1971; Qureshi and Walker 1989). However, as Figure 6.2 shows, as far as European senior citizens themselves are concerned, the family *is* less willing to care for older relatives. This finding is of the utmost importance, not only because it flies in the face of the objective evidence but also because it points to a worrying belief among older people themselves. True, a more specialized survey might have distinguished between 'families in general' and the older person's own family, but there was not space to do that.

As can be seen from Figure 6.2, the strongest views concerning the declining willingness of the family to care were expressed in France, Portugal, Italy and

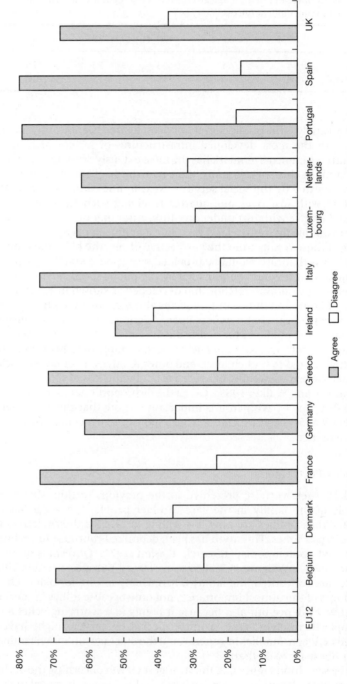

Figure 6.2 Responses to the question 'Families are less willing to care for older relatives than they used to be' (older people only).

Spain. On the other hand the strongest disagreements were in Denmark, Ireland and the UK. There was very little variation on the basis of either age or sex.

Community care

It is not mere coincidence that, as the cost of residential care has risen, policy makers throughout Europe have become more and more interested in keeping older people in their own homes or (in the most basic definition of the term as ageing in place) community care. There are other good reasons for such a policy, none more so than the expressed preference of older people themselves to remain in their own homes. This issue was put to the general public in the Eurobarometer survey by asking the following question: 'Some say that older people needing personal care should go into residential/nursing homes, while others say that the social services should help them to remain in their own homes for as long as possible. Which comes closest to your opinion?'

The vast majority (80 per cent) of the general public (90 per cent of those that expressed an opinion) thought that older people should be helped to remain in their own homes. The only countries where more than one-fifth chose the residential option were Denmark and Portugal (27 per cent). This indicated that there is strong support for community care among the general populations of the member states. Furthermore, this consensus extended across virtually the whole of the age range and was shared by both sexes. The only partial exception was among those aged 15–24, where a slightly higher proportion (18 per cent) than other age groups supported the use of residential care, but this declined among the 25–34 group to 12 per cent, where it remained more or less through to the 65 and over age group.

There is not space to do more than note in passing that some one in ten of the samples of the general public aged 15 and over in EU countries were providing care to someone within their own household as a result of a long-term illness, disability or old age. In addition, one in seven were providing out-of-house care.

Clients or consumers?

One of the most contentious current issues surrounding the long-term care of older people is whose voice should prevail in determining the provision of care? Of course, for most younger adults this sort of question does not arise: they are used to deciding for themselves what is in their own best interests. But in the care of older people a practice has developed whereby they become, in effect, the clients of professionals or quasi-professionals and these groups may decide which sort of care is appropriate for them, sometimes in discussion with informal carers.

This may have the effect of disenfranchising older people from making crucial decisions about their own lives (one of the Latin roots of 'client', a term that is much used in the social services, translates into: 'to hear, to obey'). This is a gross simplification, not least because professionals often make strenuous efforts to consult and do what is best for older people and they have the task of

Table 6.2 Who is the best person to decide on services for older people?

	EU12	B	DK	F	G	GR	IRL	I	L	NL	P	SP	UK
A relative or close friend	27.8	24.0	24.8	25.7	20.0	37.8	41.5	30.9	25.7	18.7	38.6	38.4	29.6
Older person	33.7	43.0	48.1	34.9	45.4	35.0	22.3	18.2	33.0	32.7	22.6	36.1	29.8
The service provider	5.5	8.1	9.0	3.7	3.7	8.7	5.8	7.5	5.6	11.7	14.1	3.8	4.3
Another professional (e.g. doctor)	30.2	22.3	17.0	34.7	28.5	16.9	26.8	42.2	30.1	33.4	24.0	16.6	30.6

assessing priorities for resource allocation as well as ensuring that care is provided, and it would be wrong to misread this as impugning the usually honourable motives of social services professionals. However, the matter of the human right of older people to self-determination is one that cannot easily be side-stepped (Thursz *et al.* 1995). We raised it in the general Eurobarometer survey in terms of the person in the best position to decide on the most appropriate services for older people needing long-term care. The results, in Table 6.2, show older people themselves gaining the highest vote overall, but only just, with professionals (which should be read as meaning doctors) and relatives/friends close behind. In all countries except Italy the combined percentages for the older person and their relatives or friends came to more than half the total.

Paying for care

The final part of this chapter focuses on how the long-term care of increasing numbers of frail and older people should be financed. At present in EU countries this is either provided by the state, free or at subsidized rates, or privately, paid for by the individuals concerned or by the state. As we noted earlier, Germany has recently introduced a public insurance scheme for long-term care and the issue has been debated in several other countries. We put to the general public a series of possible methods of financing long-term care and asked them to choose which they think is the best way.

The results, shown in Figure 6.3, reveal a surprisingly widespread opposition to the use of the private sector in this field. More than seven out of ten favoured either a compulsory public insurance scheme or a public service financed through taxation, and if the 'don't knows' are excluded this rose to just under eight out of ten. The citizens of Europe have spoken with clear voices on this issue: either the public sector should organize the financing of long-term care or it should both finance and provide it. There was hardly any deviation from the picture shown in Figure 6.3 on the basis of age or sex, though the group aged 55–64 was slightly more likely than others to favour compulsory public insurance.

The new member states

As we noted in Chapter 1, the research upon which this book is based derives from the European Observatory reports which were undertaken during the European Year of Older People and Solidarity Between the Generations 1993. We intend here to supplement this material by providing a brief overview of the care of older people in the three new EU states, Sweden, Austria and Finland.

Sweden and Finland present similar scenarios. Both had highly developed care systems based upon high levels of guaranteed statutory service, combined with payments for care which went beyond the merely symbolic as often is the case in other EU countries. However, since the 1980s, new mechanisms have been put into effect which have placed a greater emphasis upon familial care supported by a cash benefit structure. The strategy adopted has sought to

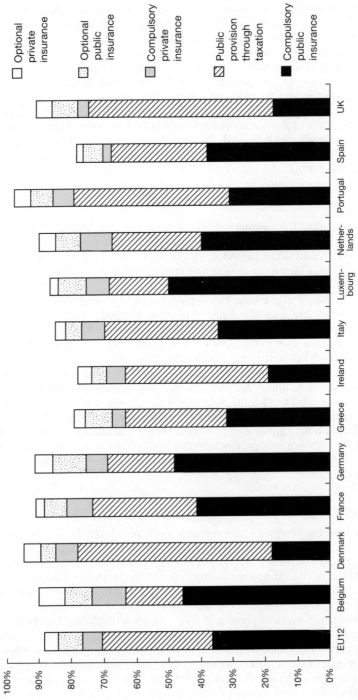

Figure 6.3 Which way forward for long-term care of older people?

maintain public service provision yet reduce its coverage through increased control of resources and greater use of informal care from families (Evers and Leichsenring 1994). For example, in 1980, 30 per cent of those aged 65 and over received formal care (e.g. home helps, long-term care). By 1991 this figure had been reduced to 21 per cent, with the largest decrease occurring in home help provision (down from 22 per cent to 16 per cent) (*Ageing International* 1995c). Thus the bulk of the funding has been passed down the decision making structures from the county councils to the municipalities. They now have the primary role of providing care-based solutions, through either service-oriented care (e.g. formal respite care) or cash-based incentives through transfers.

In Austria the structure of community care has also been subject to reform. Previously the system was very undeveloped, with heavy reliance upon family care, in both cash and kind. Over 70 per cent of care was within the informal sector, and was mostly undertaken by families (Badelt and Holzmann 1993). The system of health care was based upon a social insurance structure and, although covering the majority of the population, often did not provide for long-term care, that is, care beyond 'medical nursing' (Badelt and Holzmann 1993).

Most institutional care for older people in Austria is provided either by governmental organizations or by the voluntary sector/non-profit institutions (Badelt and Holzmann 1993). However, public funds were withdrawn from people who were deemed to have chronic conditions (i.e. beyond 'medical nursing'), and who then had to resort to private means (and their families) or means-tested social welfare payments. As recently as 1993, Austria implemented a system of non-means-tested 'comprehensive attendance allowance', which follows similar initiatives in the provinces of Tyrol, Vorarlberg and Upper Austria (Badelt and Holzmann 1993). This provides payments at seven rates, increasing in monetary value depending upon the nature and severity of the person's disability. The aim of this policy is to provide people with choice in the type of care they receive. Although this must be considered an improvement, the system of care still relies ultimately upon the family, particularly in the rural areas (Evers and Leichsenring 1994).

7

The politics of ageing societies

In this penultimate chapter, some of the loose ends of the previous discussion are pulled together. This chapter also focuses upon the policy system and attempts to offer an assessment of the degree to which older people contribute to political life in general, the extent of their presence, and of their integration into policy-making structures and organizations. We also reflect upon the extent to which there is a perceived need for further government and EU action towards and for older people. As in previous chapters, we also review the findings from the expert reports to the European Observatory and present the findings from the Eurobarometer surveys. As we have endeavoured to demonstrate in the previous chapters, the degree of social integration of older people, their involvement in a broad range of societal interactions, is linked to their personal income and other resources they have available. This in turn is set by a variety of social determinants including class, 'race' and gender as well as their personal health. This underlines the very important fact that older people should not be considered as a homogeneous mass but as a disparate group of people.

Politics and the media

It was established in Chapter 2 that senior citizens are, by and large, involved in current affairs but, while there is evidence of a considerable interest in politics, levels of active engagement in political or pressure-group activities are very low. In the parallel Eurobarometer study of the general populations of the member states, respondents were asked about the involvement of older people in politics and the media. With regard to television and radio the general public, by a large majority, were of the opinion that older people are not represented fully enough: 53 per cent compared with 33 per cent who thought they are. In Belgium, Germany, Greece, Italy and Spain some three out of five of the general public thought that older people do not figure enough in television and radio.

With regard to political life there was a slight majority of the general public saying that older people are not playing a full enough part (46 per cent as opposed to 43 per cent). This opinion was expressed by most people in Belgium (65 per cent), Spain (60 per cent) and the Netherlands (56 per cent) and was denied by most in Greece (75 per cent), France and Luxembourg (54 per cent) and Italy (50 per cent). Of course the paradox underlying this question is that throughout the EU, and indeed worldwide, many of those who are prominent political figures may be older people, yet the mass of senior citizens are often far less active in politics than their younger counterparts.

Taking this issue a stage further, the general public was asked if older people should stand up more actively for their own rights. The results, shown in Figure 7.1, indicate that this is another matter on which the people of Europe see eye to eye, with over 80 per cent of those questioned agreeing with the question. There was virtually no deviation from this across the different age groups, though there was a tendency for the proportions agreeing strongly to rise with age up to the 55–64 age group, after which there was a slight decline.

Looking at this issue from a party political perspective and bearing in mind the development of 'age-interest' politics in the USA, we wondered whether older people would join a political party formed specifically to further their own age group's interests. Perhaps remarkably, the majority were opposed to the idea but the minority – 22 per cent on average across the 12 countries sampled – seemed surprisingly large. The country-by-country breakdown is shown in Figure 7.2.

It is interesting to note that the southern European states in the Union (in Greece and Italy a third of those questioned expressed a favourable response and in Portugal over 40 per cent) all had higher positive percentages than the northern states, where between about ten and 20 per cent agreed. There could be a number of issues here which require a more thorough analysis, ranging from differences in the political process, the conceptualization of the notion of a 'civic culture', through to a greater concern with older people's everyday social and economic position which might be considered outside of party politics. However, the low percentages overall either indicate an apathy towards the more formalized political process on the part of older people or a feeling that pressure-group action around single issues (as happened recently in several EU countries, including the UK) is more effective.

Political action and older people

Despite the relatively low levels of direct participation revealed in the survey, there are signs that older people are on the move politically, an indication perhaps that they are seeking their own, bottom-up, routes to social integration. Political parties or new age-based groupings and radical 'grey panther' style movements have been formed in Belgium, Denmark, Italy, Germany, the Netherlands, Portugal and the UK. In contrast, in other countries of the Union, for example Luxembourg and Spain, the recent upsurge in political activity among pensioners has been channelled through more

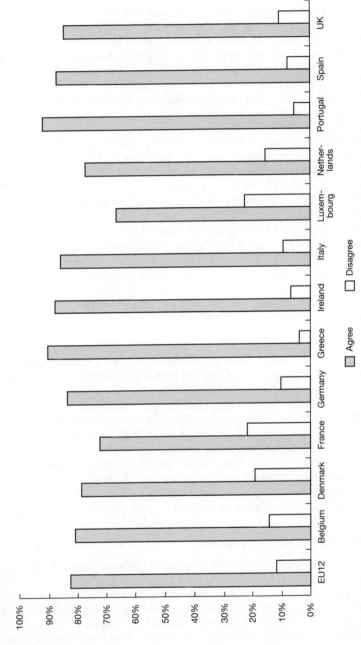

Figure 7.1 Responses to the question 'Older people should stand up more actively for their rights' ('don't knows' not shown).

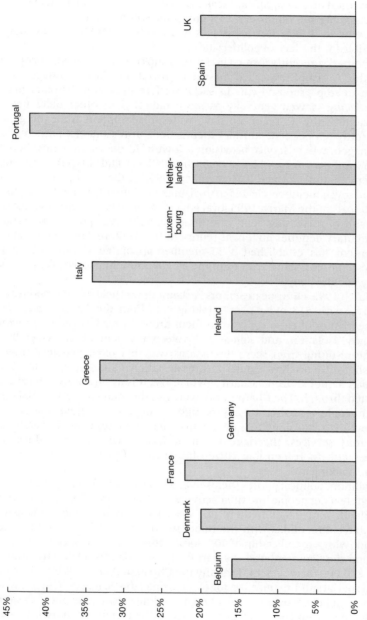

Figure 7.2 Proportion of older people who said they would join a political party formed to further their interests.

conventional pressure groups and trade union organizations. It is only in Greece and Ireland that the politicization of ageing issues does not seem to have occurred on any significant scale. The comment from the Irish expert that 'Old people are too often seen as a group for whom things get done, not as people who do things for themselves or for others' (O'Shea 1993) may be responsible for this lack of politicization.

In Denmark a recently formed pressure group comprised of older people and called the 'C Team' has called mass demonstrations, in Copenhagen, in an attempt to stop proposed cuts in social welfare provision for older people. Despite being viewed generally as more radical than other older people's organizations, the 'C Team' do have widespread support from the general public (only ten per cent consider their actions unreasonable) particularly in Copenhagen, where service provision is lowest. In the Netherlands there are two political parties for older people, the UNIE-55 and the AOV (Algemeen Ouderenverbond), formed in September 1993. In the 1994 general election they had seven members elected to the Dutch parliament, and followed this up with 30 seats in the March 1995 local government elections. However, largely as a result of increasing debts and disagreements over policy, the national parliamentary deputies no longer represent the AOV. In Austria the national government has established a 35-member appointed Council of Seniors (Bundessenioren), which can examine all governmental legislative proposals relating to older people.

In March 1992 a European Seniors Parliament was held in Luxembourg over two days, with 518 older people taking part from the 12 EU states. They discussed issues of close concern to them around four key themes: income, autonomy, isolation, and solidarity between the generations. Overall, the message resulting from these discussions was that older people wanted to establish, for themselves, similar forums at national and European level. The European Senior Citizen's Charter, which has this as one of its central aims, was voted through. The Charter also expresses the individual and social rights of older people. It further stresses the rights to dignity, autonomy and security of income; to housing; to safe environments; to residential, health and community services; the right to pursue leisure, cultural and educational activities and to responsible citizenship through effective participation in decision-making processes.

In addition, political parties themselves are beginning to recognize the need to integrate older people into their activities and structures. For instance, in the Netherlands and Belgium there are special groups within existing parties which have direct links with the trade unions. In Austria the Pensionisten-verband (with a membership of 300,000) is affiliated to the Social Democratic Party and the Seniorenbund is a part of the Austrian People's Party and has nearly 250,000 members. In Germany the Christian Democrats established, in 1988, a special sub-organization for older people, the 'Senioren-Union', which is open to all people over the age of 60, including existing members. A similar development is noted in the German Social Democratic Party, which has a network of senior circles (Seniorenarbeitskreise). Indeed, Trude Unrah, then leader of the age-based party 'Die Grauen', sat in parliament for three years up to 1990.

Education in the third age

In the field of education we have seen the rapid spread in Europe of universities of the third age (U3A), designed to reintegrate older people into the world of higher education. This development is of the greatest importance because it is aimed at overcoming the education deficit experienced by many older people, especially older women (Coopmans *et al.* 1988; Dooghe and Appleton 1995). For example, Italy has around 50,000 older people registered for courses under its university of the third age. These 'Golden Age Universities' are concentrated in the northern Italian cities and have been set up with the specific aim of preventing the marginalization of older people in Italian society and encouraging older people to learn.

In France, the Université de Troisiéme Age (UtA) was founded in Toulouse in 1973 by Pierre Vellas. Since that time UtAs have spread throughout France, and by 1991 there were over 40 such universities. The French UtAs not only provide university courses for older people but also run workshops and conferences. Although such institutions are dominated by mainly middle-class and younger senior citizens (a fact which is true across all 15 countries of the EU) they have encouraged greater social integration by bringing this group back into the formal educational process and into contact with younger people. Similar universities of the third age are found in Belgium, the Netherlands and, to a lesser extent, in the UK.

However, in Belgium, older people have to pay a nominal charge to become a member of U3A, which may restrict their access to education. Similarly, in Germany and Denmark, although further and adult education is widely available, participation by older people themselves is small (87 per cent of Danes over the age of 70 stated that they never participated in educational activities) (Platz 1989). Many of these courses are held in the evening, when fear of being exposed to violent crime is greatest, particularly on the part of women (Sørensen 1988). In Spain there is little information on the participation of older people in education. However, there is a higher level of illiteracy among older women in Spain as a result of the traditionally low priority given to the education of women. In Greece, KAPI members are provided with opportunities for adult education. Portugal, however, represents a stark contrast to the other EU states in this area. It is unique in having a very high percentage of older people who are illiterate. A survey (in 1981) indicated that over 50 per cent of people over the age of 65 were illiterate and that this figure increased to 60 per cent for older women. These high illiteracy rates act as a constraint on the full social integration of Portugeuse older people, especially women.

Older people and political activity in the UK

Having considered the contributions made by older people to political life in general in the EU, we now focus upon the situation in the UK. Older people, in particular those over the state pension age, are usually regarded as a homogeneous entity by the political system in the UK, an attitude heightened by the application of a definitive pension age. The very act of withdrawing people from making a positive contribution through their economic activity by the application of a fixed pension age also disengages them from contacts made while in work (work colleagues, involvement in trade unions and so on) and reduces the opportunities for greater social inclusion.

Significantly, as was noted in Chapter 5, the trend has been for even earlier disengagement than official pension and retirement ages stipulate, through redundancy and unemployment (which for many older people has become a euphemism for retirement) and the government-run Job Release Scheme (between 1977 and 1988) which 'allowed' early exit for workers if their job was taken by an unemployed person (Laczko and Phillipson 1991).

Yet older people have an important role in the formal structures operating in the UK. For example, most High Court judges are over the age of 50, as are the leaders of the larger trade unions, many high-profile politicians, and representatives from the main employers' organization, the Confederation of British Industry (CBI). However, as Walker (1986) has indicated, in the post-war period there has been no overt politics of old age in UK. Until very recently there was consensus between the main political parties about the deservingness of the pensioners' cause, and the grass-roots organizations tended to focus on purely local issues. Thus one British commentator has suggested that 'the activity of pensioners' organizations is not linked to sustained examination of actions by government in the post-war period' (Miles 1994: 4).

There is an increasing number of local pensioners' action groups (e.g. Strathclyde Pensioners Forum, Sheffield Pensioners Action Group, Greater London Forum for the Elderly, Association of Greater London Older Women (AGLOW)) as well as nationally organized ones (e.g. Association of Retired Persons, Older Feminists Network, Campaign for Equal State Pension Ages (CESPA), the Growing Old Disgracefully Network, National Federation of Retirement Pensions Associations and the National Pensioners Convention) and the 'retired' sections of the larger trade unions (e.g. TGWU, AEEU and GMB) which are coordinated under the British Pensioners and Trade Unions Action Association (Ginn 1993). However, until recently the political activity and militancy of these organizations operated on a limited scale in terms of both numbers and influence within the policy-making system. Recently this has begun to change, particularly following the reconstitution of the National Pensioners' Convention in 1989. Political activity coalesced around the single issue of the government's proposal to impose a VAT rate of 17.5 per cent on fuel bills and resulted in a mass lobby of parliament which helped to stop the second stage of the VAT increase (from eight to 17.5 per cent).

Grass-roots political action by pensioners flows from one of the main concerns of most pensioners in all EU countries (see Chapter 4): their living standards and, especially, the size of their state pensions. In British social attitudes surveys conducted by Social and Community Planning Research (SCPR) since 1983 (Brooks *et al.* 1992), pensioners have consistently expressed dissatisfaction with the level of the state pension. For example, when asked if they felt that the state pension was adequate or not, 66 per cent in 1983 rising to 77 per cent in 1989 felt that it was low or very low. Furthermore, they expected its real value to diminish over time (45.1 per cent) and 62.4 per cent in the 1989 sample indicated that they expected to purchase less in the following year with their state pension (Brooks *et al.* 1992).

Such widespread concern over the diminishing level of their pension has not been translated yet into any determined political action to alter the situation. For example, there are no significant political parties specifically for and organized by older people as in the Netherlands and Germany. Perhaps this is due to the problems associated with organizing such a large and disparate group. The recent debacle over the theft of funds from Mirror Group Newspapers has pushed those concerned into political action to alter the law (and enacted as the Pensions Act 1995) to protect such occupational pension funds following the recommendations from the Goode Committee inquiry into the affair.

Voting patterns

At the last general election, in 1992, support for the two main political parties (Conservative and Labour) in Britain among the over-50s was broadly equal in percentage terms. A study undertaken by Midwinter for the Carnegie Inquiry indicated that 46 per cent of those over 55 voted for the Conservative Party, 34 per cent for Labour and 17 per cent for the Liberal Democrats (Carnegie Institute 1993: 89). However, when considering support for each party among women over 55, that for Labour was at the same level as at the last election in 1987, despite their electoral gains in 1992. On the other hand, support for the Conservatives by women over 55 increased 'by as much as five per cent' (Rallings and Thrasher 1992: 1). This is somewhat of a paradox, since it is older women rather than men who face an increasing likelihood of poverty in their later life (as we noted in Chapter 4) yet they still vote for the political party which has cut the value of the state pension.

Confirmation of Rallings and Thrasher's (1992) findings are reflected in surveys conducted before the election (Gallup 1992) which indicated that support for the two parties among men over 60 was evenly balanced, whereas older women identified with the Conservative Party (Walker 1986). Both women and men in this age group are strongly committed to one of the two parties. The Gallup survey asked interviewees whether they identified strongly or only moderately with their chosen political party. Those aged over 65 demonstrated the highest percentages for strong identification among the whole sample (54 per cent), and 80 per cent of those over 45 years had decided whom to vote for 'a long time ago' (more than three weeks).

The 1993 European Year

Finally, older people in the special Eurobarometer survey were asked about the European Year of Older People and Solidarity Between the Generations and, specifically, what subjects they would like to be better informed about. The results exposed a widespread interest in 1993 and in being better informed about benefits and services available in both their own and other EU countries.

First of all, only 14 per cent said that they did *not* want to be better informed about the European Year and related issues. Then, over half (54 per cent) of the

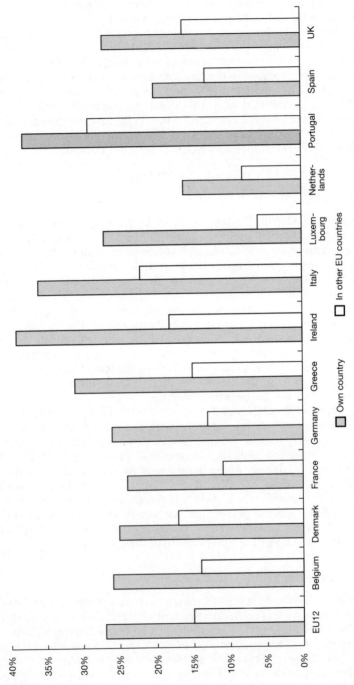

Figure 7.3 Percentages wanting to be better informed about how older people organize themselves and make their views known in their own country and in other EU countries (percentages not exclusive).

older people sampled wanted to be better informed about the benefits, services and facilities available to older people in their own country. The proportions wanting this information were at their highest in Portugal (70 per cent) and the former GDR (72 per cent) and at their lowest in Luxembourg (38 per cent) and the Netherlands (36 per cent). One-quarter of older people wanted information about benefits, services and facilities available in other EU countries. This interest peaked in Portugal (38 per cent) and the UK (34 per cent) and slumped in the Netherlands (nine per cent). These data suggest a remarkably high proportion of older people with an interest in provision in other EU countries. This impression was confirmed by the fact that just over one in five expressed a desire to be better informed about what the European Commission is doing to encourage solidarity between the generations. Interest in this was at its highest in Portugal (32 per cent), Italy (29 per cent) and France (27 per cent), and lowest in Spain (14 per cent).

Responses to this question also confirmed the latent interest of older people in political activity. Thus more than a quarter wanted to be better informed about how older people organize themselves and make their views known in their own country, and some 15 per cent wanted similar information about other EU countries (Figure 7.3). Additionally, some 15 per cent of older people wanted to learn about how they could actually take part in the activities and events organized as part of the European Year. This may seem like a small proportion, but if their interest was translated into actual participation it would have meant something of the order of nine million people actively involved in the European Year.

The question does remain as to how successful the European Year was in raising awareness of issues and concerns of older people and encouraging solidarity between the generations. In the UK, a market research company (NOP) was commissioned by the UK government to answer just this question (Department of Health 1995). They interviewed 1724 people over the age of 15 between 9 and 14 February 1994, shortly after the end of the Year. The results were disappointing, with two-thirds of respondents indicating that they did not know or could not remember what the focus of 1993 was. Another disappointing result indicated that only one in ten of the adult population had consciously been aware of the European Year. Yet looking at these responses in a more positive light, such a figure represents over four million adults across the 12 countries of the EU who *had* realized that 1993 had been the European Year. This in itself is significant.

Also, these results reflect the UK government's reticence in publicizing the Year effectively compared with several other EU governments. This may be seen in the responses given to the NOP survey question as to whether subjects had seen or heard about the Year or seen the distinctive logo. The majority (84 per cent) had not heard about the Year nor had seen the logo. Only five per cent had seen the logo and only seven per cent had heard of the Year. The following year (1994) was the European Year of the Family and this received widespread press and media attention with a popularly scheduled television series devoted to the Year. Little media attention in the UK was addressed to the 1993 Year. Cynically, perhaps, the European Year of the

Family had more potential for political capital to be made than that of the European Year of Older People and Solidarity Between the Generations, especially within an ageist society.

These issues aside, the 1993 European Year overall can be seen to be a 'curate's egg'. The opinion poll cited above clearly paints a rather negative picture. Yet the Year was very successful in creating networks and in channelling resources to and enthusing those organizations with a direct interest in and for older people. For example, over 713 organizations responded to a questionnaire about their involvement in the Year. This indicated that over 8500 different activities and events were organized, ranging from competitions to meetings, conferences and similar events. Additionally, the UK European Resources Unit, which developed out of the UK Secretariat for the Year, has been established and is based at Age Concern England. The aim of this unit is to build on the impetus provided by the 1993 European Year. The seminar held at the end of the European Year at the Department of Health attempted to convey this by carrying the title 'A Great Year to Build On'.

The Year clearly failed to grab the interest and attention of the citizens of Europe as a whole. However, perhaps the International Year of the Elderly (*sic*) in 1999 will be able to excite the interest of more of the population.

8

Conclusion

The main purpose of this book is to disseminate the findings of some unique research conducted under the auspices of the Commission of the European Communities. As we noted in Chapter 1, these were the first comprehensive attempts to compare the social and economic status of older people and the attitudes of the general public towards this group across all member states of the EU and, therefore, they must be seen as preliminary analyses or ground-clearing operations. Accepting that it would be premature to try to draw definite conclusions from this unfinished research, some findings speak for themselves and some are corroborated by other evidence. Therefore in this final chapter we will draw together some tentative conclusions. In doing so we focus on the key theme that has been present throughout this book and the research on which it is based: the fundamental importance, both to the individuals concerned and to European societies, of maintaining the social integration of older people. Intergenerational solidarity in particular is an essential element in both primary (informal) and secondary (formal) relations and, therefore, crucial in the maintenance of social cohesion.

The policy deficit

There can be little doubt, from both the secondary analyses of Observatory experts and the survey of public opinion in the EU, that the level of social integration experienced by older people remains relatively high in both micro and macro forms. That is good news and should be a cause for celebration. In the Eurobarometer survey the people of Western Europe said loud and clear, for example, that older people maintain a special place as a deserving cause for action by national governments and the Union as a whole, and moreover they want more of both forms of action. It would be mistaken to see this as a display of pity for older people. The Eurobarometer findings reveal a far richer tapestry than that flimsy piece of cloth. For instance, there is proof of very powerful intergenerational solidarity between young and older workers and pensioners. True, this is partly a matter of self-interest, since younger people these days can expect to be older people some day, but none the less important for that. Then there is a widespread awareness of age discrimination in all member states and the feeling that something should be done about this injustice. Finally, there is a strong belief that older people themselves should stand up for their own rights more actively.

Turning to senior citizens themselves, they too have spoken through the medium of the Eurobarometer survey. There are signs of resentment with regard to the low level of pensions in some countries and of segregative impulses, but also proof of embededness in their families and favourable attitudes towards youth. There are disturbing indications of financial insecurity among a minority but, overall, a sense of mild satisfaction with the lives they lead, without much complaint or overt political action.

Just under one-quarter of older people were very satisfied with their lives, more than half fairly satisfied and only one in five not satisfied. The variations between countries cannot be painted over and the challenge the Union now faces is to minimize those that derive mainly from differences in socio-economic conditions. These differences may be summarized in the following statistical spiral: 68 per cent of older people in Denmark are very satisfied with the lives they lead, 43 per cent in the Netherlands, 25 per cent in Spain, six per cent in Greece and three per cent in Portugal. Conversely, only three per cent of Danish elders are not satisfied with their lives compared with 41 per cent of the Portuguese and 59 per cent of Greek elders.

How long the relative political acquiescence of older people will last in the face of such divergence is a matter for speculation, but there were indications in the Eurobarometer surveys of a latent interest in political activity, a clear impression of active engagement in current affairs, and a strong feeling among the general public that older people should stand up more actively for their rights. We noted also, in Chapter 7, the wide range of pensioner action groups, including some political parties, that have emerged all over Europe in the last ten years. The demands of these groups – for better pensions, health services, long-term care, transport and a safer environment – suggest that the European politics of old age have entered a new era, one in which conflicts over social and economic policies are becoming more overt than previously (Walker 1996).

In fact, in several EU countries, it is possible to witness already a 'policy deficit' between, on the one hand, the needs and demands of older people, supported by the general public, and, on the other, the social and economic policies of governments. In a few extreme cases the contrast is glaring between the obsessive concern of some politicians with the economic 'burden' of societal ageing and the increase in poverty among older people or the increased inequality between older and younger people. Of course, this deficit is partly explained by the economic and ideological agenda which is set by the EU's goal of economic and monetary union, as well as the prescriptions of other international economic agencies (Walker 1990). But, also we think, the research reviewed in this book demonstrates that most European governments have not come to terms with the fact that their societies are ageing and have not begun to adjust economic and political institutions to this new reality.

There were indications in the Eurobarometer surveys that, in this respect, some policy makers are out of step with the people. For example, more than three-quarters of all EU respondents thought that their government does not do enough for older people, and in only four countries – Denmark, France, Luxembourg and the Netherlands – did the majority fall below seven out of ten. Antithetically, those same four countries were the ones where the largest proportions were likely to say that the government is doing all it should (from 23 per cent in Denmark to 36 per cent in the Netherlands). There were significant differences in responses between the former FRG and GDR. For example, 82 per cent of former East Germans thought that the German government does not do enough, compared with 68 per cent of former West Germans.

There was hardly any difference between age groups in their opinions on the adequacy of current government action, with all age groups from 15-year-olds through to the over-65s agreeing by well over 70 per cent. In a similar vein respondents were asked whether the EU is doing enough with regard to older people. Predictably, the level of uncertainty increased markedly compared with the question about national governments. Thus the average of one in three who replied 'don't know' carries its own powerful message with regard to the so-called European 'democratic deficit'. This uncertainty peaked in Denmark (at 43 per cent), followed by the Netherlands and Spain (35 per cent) and declined to 18 per cent in Portugal.

The other important finding to emerge from this question is that an average of just under three out of five of those sampled said that the EU should do more for older people. If the 'don't knows' are excluded, nearly nine out of ten held this opinion. The country-by-country breakdowns are shown in Figure 8.1. There were slight tendencies both for younger people to say that the Union should do more and for older people to be more uncertain, which is a significant result by itself.

The existence of a policy deficit at national and European levels emphasizes the important distinction we made, in Chapter 3, between the social integration of older people in the primary relationships of family and neighbourhood and their experience of exclusion from some of the major economic and political institutions in their country. Therefore it is important to consider the barriers that older people are confronted with by these institutions.

Removing the barriers to social integration

Although there are positive signs of change, many older people are not integrated fully into the social and economic life of their national or local communities. These older people have yet to achieve full citizenship. This does not apply to all, because integration and exclusion are unevenly distributed among older people in all EU countries. There are four key barriers to their social integration:

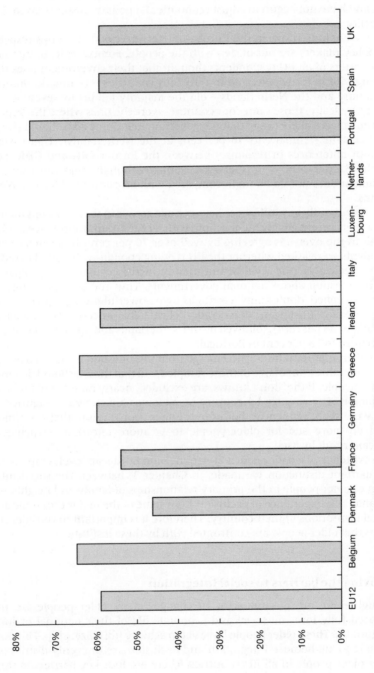

Figure 8.1 Percentages saying that the EU should do more for older people.

1 *Incomes.* If individuals have low incomes, their level of participation in social roles, relationships and forms of consumption is restricted. Poverty remains a persistent problem among a minority of older people. That minority varies from less than ten per cent in Denmark and Luxembourg to more than 50 per cent in Greece, Portugal and Spain. The Eurobarometer surveys found that only a minority of older Europeans feel financially secure. There are also significant differences in incomes between pensioners and, in the EU as a whole, older women are among those most likely to suffer poverty and deprivation. In other words, a significant minority of older Europeans lack the material basis for social integration (Chapter 4).

2 *Age discrimination.* The early-exit trend is firmly established and would be difficult to reverse. But it is one of the well-springs of age discrimination in the labour market and wider society. Age discrimination remains a formidable barrier to participation in the labour force and in other formal institutions. For example, in the UK a 1994 government survey found that age restrictions applied to 28 per cent of all advertised job vacancies, and six per cent of vacancies were closed to people over 40 and eight per cent to those over 60 (Chapter 5).

3 *Health and social care.* Some older people face physical and mental barriers to integration. The fact that older disabled people have higher levels of need than their non-disabled peers is insufficiently recognized by policy makers in all EU countries. Additionally, health and social services are rarely organized in ways that maximize participation and integration. Instead, they tend to provide hierarchically structured, minimalist services oriented towards service providers rather than being focused upon the users. It is worth remembering that, long before community care became a policy choice on cost grounds, it was advocated as a means to ensure the continued integration of older people in community life (Chapter 6).

4 *Fear.* Older people particularly fear crime. Evidence from a number of national surveys on crime demonstrates that older people are less likely than younger ones to be the victims of crime. However, there is disturbing evidence from several countries that older people feel vulnerable and this is resulting in the operation of a voluntary curfew. For example, in the Netherlands, it is reported that more than half of those aged 65 and over no longer go out after dark and in Denmark two-fifths of women aged 60 and over are afraid of being exposed to violence in the evening.

These barriers to social integration highlight the central role of social and economic policies in creating the conditions for older people to become fully participating senior citizens. Of vital and primary importance is the provision of an adequate income for *all* older people, but in particular older women. At the very least, the extreme forms of exclusion associated with poverty should be abolished. Combating age discrimination in the labour market would assist senior citizens' access to employment and help redefine the meaning of age in society as a whole. Action on crime prevention, particularly in inner-city areas, would begin to remove the fear that prevents some older people from participating in social activities. Finally, an increase in home care services and a new model of service provision that enables older people to exercise greater power and influence would help to promote social integration. Also, by placing an emphasis on the promotion of intergenerational solidarity, policy makers could raise awareness about the vital importance of harmony between the generations.

This, in outline, is a strategy to promote the social integration of older people in their local and national communities – to create the conditions for greater participation and full citizenship, if older people themselves choose to take up this opportunity. But, as noted earlier, the climate in which social integration is being sought is sometimes a hostile one. Budget deficits and various proposals in EU countries to reduce public expenditure on pensions, health and social services are not, on the face of it, conducive to the promotion of social integration. And yet, for once, the interests of all of the key stakeholders may be synchronized to some extent.

The sophisticated application of a concept of 'productive ageing' could, in the long term, assist in containing pension and health care costs (where 'production' means not only paid employment but unpaid activities such as voluntary work, family labour, self-care and services for friends and neighbours). This is the great challenge facing all EU countries: the creation of new, more active images and roles for older citizens, commensurate with the changing realities of our ageing societies. In practice, this means nothing less than the re-definition of old age in policy and practice. The prize for achieving this transformation is enormous. Tapping the massive resources of talent in the third and fourth ages, for example by bringing excluded older workers back in from the cold, would ensure the transmission of values and skills from one generation to the next. It would also maintain high levels of solidarity between the generations and ensure that all older people achieve the minimum European standards required for human dignity. At the same time, these measures would positively assist in containing the costs of pensions and health care.

Of course, European societies should aspire to no less. However, if there is resistance to change on the part of national policy makers, they should not be surprised if older people no longer conform to the passive images of previous decades. Senior citizens are becoming more active and are beginning to seize the initiative for themselves. In the end, it is likely to be pressure from older people themselves, through active political participation, that is likely to create the conditions for their own social integration. In ageing societies it is in everyone's interest to promote the full citizenship of older people.

Appendix I

Members of the Observatory on Ageing and Older People

Belgium	Olgierd Kuty (University of Liége)
Denmark	Merete Platz (Danish National Institute of Social Research, Copenhagen)
France	Anne-Marie Guillemard (University of Paris I (Sorbonne))
Germany	Jens Alber (University of Konstanz)
Greece	Dimitris Ziomas (National Centre of Social Research, Athens)
Ireland	Eamon O'Shea (University College, Galway)
Italy	Aurelia Florea (Institute for the Study of Social Services, Rome)
Luxembourg	Gaston Schàber (Centre for Population, Poverty and Socio-Economic Policies, Walferdange)
Netherlands	Kees Knipscheer (Free University, Amsterdam)
Portugal	Heloisa Perista (Centre for the Study of Social Interventions, Lisbon)
Spain	Juan Antonio Cordón (Institute of Demography, Madrid)
United Kingdom	Alan Walker (University of Sheffield)

Appendix II

Summary of the European Commission's decision on support for actions in favour of older people

This proposal has the support of the Economic and Social Committee of the EU, the European Parliament and the Commission. Its main purpose is to seek a 'special one-off follow-up initiative' to build upon and extend the many successes of the 1993 European Year of Older People and Solidarity Between the Generations. One of the successes it specifically mentions is the exchange of practical information and experience on matters concerning ageing in Europe. It also attaches great importance to the continuing cooperation between those NGOs, institutions, charitable associations and foundations which have a special interest in furthering social welfare and social policy towards older people.

The preamble then notes the 'considerable economic and social implications' of the ageing of the population in Europe and the effects that this trend will have upon the economic and social policy of member states and more generally, the EU as a whole. More specifically, it singles out the implications for the employment market, social security and social expenditure. In the light of this, the proposal calls for greater cooperation and consultation between the Commission, member states and the representatives of older people, with the aim of strengthening social 'solidarity within the EU'.

In the light of these facts, Article 1 calls for a framework to meet the challenges of an ageing Europe for a period of just over four years from September 1995, with Article 2 identifying the three principal objectives for this period. These seek a strengthening of solidarity between generations and an improvement in the social integration of older people with the aim of developing the 'role and potential' of the 'active retired'. It is suggested that the social integration of older migrants, disabled older people, older people living in remote areas and older women are of special significance and should be considered a priority. With these in mind and drawing on reports from the EU Observatory, the proposal calls for the development of 'best practice' in the following areas:

1 the improvement of the situation of older women,
2 the transition from work to retirement,
3 the management of an ageing workforce,
4 the care and access to care for dependent older people.

Article 3 specifies the manner in which the objectives mentioned in Article 2 shall be achieved. These are identified as projects with a specific focus upon the objectives of Article 2 as well as comparative and 'trans-national initiatives' promoting exchange of experience, information and 'best practice'. It calls for these to be developed as partnerships between public and private institutions, as well as professional and voluntary organizations. It also seeks the continuation of regular reports on the socio-economic situation of older people in Europe produced through the research of independent 'experts' from the European Observatory on Ageing and Older People.

Articles 4–7 refer to the funding criteria, the method of implementation of the proposal and the responsibility of the Commission for dissemination of information emanating from the actions identified in the proposal. Article 8 calls for a presentation (before 31 December 2000) of a report on the implementation and results of the actions to the Council of the European Parliament.

Appendix III

Technical specifications of the Eurobarometer surveys

Eurobarometer 37.1 (general public)

The Eurobarometer 37.1 covered the population of the respective nationalities, aged 15 years and over, in each of the member states of the EU. The basic sample design applied in all member states was a multi-stage, random (probability) one. In each country, a number of sampling points was drawn with probability proportional to population size (for a total coverage of the country) and to population density.

The points were drawn systematically from all 'administrative regional units', after stratification by individual unit and type of area. They thus represent the whole territory of the member states according to EUROSTAT and according to the distribution of the national, resident population in terms of metropolitan, urban and rural areas. In each of the selected sampling points, a starting address was drawn, at random. Further addresses were selected as every *n*th address by standard random route procedures; from the initial address in each household, the respondent was drawn, at random. All interviews were face to face in people's homes and in the appropriate national language. The total number of interviews achieved in each country, the survey organizations responsible for carrying out the field work and the field work dates are contained in Table AIII.1.

For each country a comparison between the sample and the 'universe' was carried out. The universe description was derived from EUROSTAT population data. For all member states a national weighting procedure, using marginal and intercellular weighting, was carried out based on this universe description. In all countries, sex, age, region and size of locality were introduced in the iteration procedure. For international weighting (i.e. EU averages), INRA (EUROPE) applies the official population figures as published by EUROSTAT in the *Regional Statistics Yearbook* of 1988. The total population figures for input in this post-weighting procedure are listed in Table AIII.1.

Survey results are *estimations*, the accuracy of which, everything being equal, rests upon the sample size and upon the observed percentage. With samples of about 1000 interviews, the real percentages vary within the confidence limits shown in Table AIII.2.

Table AIII.1 Eurobarometer 37.1: survey details

Countries	Institutes	No. of interviews	Field work dates	Population 15+ (×1000)
Belgium	Marketing Unit	1017	21/04–09/05	7,994.4
Denmark	GFK Danmark	1000	21/04–07/05	4,160.4
Germany (East)	Sample Institut	1058	21/04–29/04	13,607.0
Germany (West)	Sample Institut	1008	21/04–09/05	51,708.0
Greece	Keme	1000	20/04–19/05	7,825.6
Spain	ICP/Research	1000	20/04–08/05	29,427.2
France	TMO Consultants	1003	21/04–04/05	43,318.5
Ireland	Lansdowne Market Research	1043	21/04–12/05	2,583.0
Italy	Pragma	1046	21/04–13/05	45,902.8
Luxembourg	Ilres	498	21/04–18/05	302.6
The Netherlands	NIPO	1002	23/04–10/5	11,603.6
Portugal	NORMA	1000	24/04–12/05	7,718.7
Great Britain	MAI International Market Research	1062	20/04–07/05	44,562.0
Northern Ireland	Ulster Marketing Services	304	21/04–11/05	1,159.1

Table AIII.2   Eurobarometer 37.1: sample confidence limits

Observed percentages	Confidence limits
10% or 90%	±1.9%
20% or 80%	±2.5%
30% or 70%	±2.7%
40% or 60%	±3.0%
50%	±3.1%

Eurobarometer 37.2 (older people only)

The Eurobarometer 37.2 covered the population of the respective nationalities, aged 60 years and over, in each of the member states. The basic sample design applied in all member states was a multi-stage quota sample. In each country, a number of sampling points was drawn with probability proportional to the (total) population size (for a total coverage of the country) and to (total) population density.

Sampling procedures followed those for Eurobarometer 37.1, outlined above, except that in each household the respondent was drawn based on quota instructions. Quotas were derived from national census statistics, or from EUROSTAT population data (1 January 1990). As in 37.1, all interviews were face to face in people's homes and in the appropriate national language and the same survey companies were used. The total number of interviews achieved in each country, the survey organizations responsible for carrying out the field work and the field work dates are contained in Table AIII.3.

Similar post-weighting procedures were used to those in the 37.1 survey: sex × marital status; sex × age; region and size of locality. The total population figures (60 years and over) used in this procedure are listed in Table AIII.3.

Again, survey results are estimations, the accuracy of which rests upon the sample size, the probability level required and the observed percentage. With samples of about

Table AIII.3   Eurobarometer 37.2: survey details

Countries	No. of interviews	Field work dates	Population 60+
Belgium	421	21/04–13/05	1,824,764
Denmark	411	21/04–13/05	1,004,598
Germany (East)	456	20/04–13/04	2,984,937
Germany (West)	437	21/04–09/05	12,246,800
Greece	400	28/04–19/05	1,649,455
Spain	400	23/04–08/05	5,833,269
France	405	21/04–07/05	9,544,920
Ireland	447	21/04–16/05	508,220
Italy	402	21/04–13/05	9,850,763
Luxembourg	209	23/04–17/05	56,349
The Netherlands	409	22/04–02/05	2,276,194
Portugal	401	25/04–10/05	1,557,747
Great Britain	405	20/04–09/05	11,014,954

Table AIII.4   Eurobarometer 37.2: sample confidence
limits

Observed percentages	Confidence limits
5% or 95%	±2.1%
10% or 90%	±2.9%
20% or 80%	±3.9%
30% or 70%	±4.5%
40% or 60%	±4.8%
50%	±4.9%

400 interviews, the real percentages vary within the confidence limits (at 95% probability level) shown in Table AIII.4.

All Eurobarometer data files are stored at the Zentral Archiv (Universität Köln, Bachemer Strasse, 40, D-5000 Köln 41). They are at the disposal of all institutes that are members of the European Consortium for Political Research (Essex), of the Inter-University Consortium for Political and Social Research (Michigan) and of all those interested in social science research. The results of the Eurobarometer surveys are analysed and made available through the Unit 'Surveys, Research, Analyses' of DG X of the Commission of the EU, Rue de la Loi 200, B-1049, Brussels.

References

Age Concern (1991) *Discontinuing Care*. London: Age Concern.

Ageing International (1995a) Hospice catches on. *Ageing International*, September: 6.

Ageing International (1995b) Extendiendo la mano. *Ageing International*, September: 15.

Ageing International (1995c) Women hard hit by cuts in formal care. *Ageing International*, September: 7.

Alber, J. (1993) The social integration of older people in Germany, in A. Walker (ed.) *Older People in Europe: Social Integration*. Brussels: CEC.

Andersson, L. (1993) *Elderly in Sweden and Europe*. Stockholm: The National Board of Health and Welfare.

Andersson, L. and Sundström, G. (1996) Social networks of elderly people in Sweden, in H. Liturin (ed.) *The Social Networks of Older People: A Cross-National Analysis*. New York: Praeger.

Anson, Sir J. (1996) *Pensions: 2000 and Beyond. The Report of the Retirement Income Inquiry, Vol. 1*. London: Recruitment Income Inquiry.

Arber, S. and Ginn, J. (1991) *Gender and Later Life*. London: Sage.

Arber, S. and Ginn, J. (1995) Connecting gender and ageing: a new beginning? in S. Arber and J. Ginn (eds) *Connecting Gender and Ageing: A Sociological Approach*. Buckingham: Open University Press.

Atkinson, A.B. (1991) *The Development of State Pensions in the United Kingdom*, STICERD, Welfare State Programme Paper No. 58. London: LSE.

Audit Commission (1992) *Community Care: Managing the Cascade of Change*. London: HMSO.

Badelt, C. and Holzmann, A. (1993) Care for the elderly in Austria: innovative projects on the local level, in A. Evers and I. Svetlik (eds) *Balancing Pluralism*. Aldershot: Avebury/Vienna: European Centre.

Bengston, V. and Achenbaum, W.A. (eds) (1993) *The Changing Contract Across the Generations*. New York: Aldine.

Bernard, M. and Meade, K. (1993) A third age lifestyle for older women? in M. Bernard and K. Meade (eds) *Women Come of Age*. London: Edward Arnold.

Bosanquet, N., Laing, W. and Propper, C. (1990) *Elderly Consumers in Britain: Europe's Poor Relations?* London: Laing and Buisson.

Brooks, L., Hedges, S,. Jowell, R., Lewis, J., Prior, G., Sebastian, G., Taylor, B. and Witherspoon, S. (1992) *British Social Attitudes Cumulative Source Book*. Aldershot: Social and Community Planning Research/Gower.

Bury, M. (1995) Ageing, gender and sociological theory, in S. Arber and J. Ginn (eds) *Connecting Gender and Ageing: A Sociological Approach*. Buckingham: Open University Press.

Butler, R., Oberlink, M. and Schecter, M. (eds) (1990) *The Promise of Productive Aging*. New York: Springer.

Calcoen, F. and Greiner, D. (1992) 'Le passage de la Vie Active a la Retraite – l'Italie', mimeo. Lille: CRESGE.

Callan, T., Nolan, B., Whelan, B. J., Hannan, D. F. and Creighton, S. (1989) *Poverty, Income and Welfare in Ireland*. Dublin: Economic and Social Research Institute.

Carnegie Institute (1993) *Life, Work and Livelihood in the Third Age: Final Report of the Carnegie Inquiry into the Third Age*. Dunfermline: Carnegie United Kingdom Trust.

Casey, B. and Laczko, F. (1989) Early retired or long term unemployed? The situation of non-working men aged 55–64 from 1979 to 1986. *Work, Employment and Society*, 3(4): 509–26.

Coopmans, M., Harrop, A. and Hermans-Huskes, M. (1988) *The Social and Economic Situation of Older Women in Europe*. Brussels: EC Commission.

Croft, C. (ed.) (1993) *European Networks of Innovative Projects Concerning Older People*. Brussels: DGV, Commission of the European Communities.

Daly, M. (1993) *Abandoned: Profile of Europe's Homeless People*. Brussels: FEANTSA.

Davies, B. and Challis, D. (1986) *Matching Resources to Needs in Community Care*. Aldershot: Gower.

Davies, B. and Ward, S. (1992) *Women and Personal Pensions*. London: HMSO.

Department of Health (1989a) *Caring for People*. London: HMSO.

Department of Health (1989b) *Working for Patients*. London: HMSO.

Department of Health (1995) *European Year – A Historical Report and Evaluation*. London: DoH.

Department of Health and Social Security (1989) *Supplementary Benefit Take-up 1985*. London: House of Commons Library.

Department of Health Social Services Inspectorate (1992) *Confronting Elder Abuse*. London: HMSO.

Department of Social Security (1996) *The Treatment of Pension Rights on Divorce*, Cm 3345. London: HMSO.

Dooghe, G. and Appleton, N. (1995) *Elderly Women in Europe: Choices and Challenges*. London: Anchor Housing.

Durkheim, E. (1952) *Suicide: A Study in Sociology*. London: Routledge and Kegan Paul.

Durkheim, E. (1993) *The Division of Labour in Society*. New York: Macmillan.

Eurostat (1994) *Labour Force Survey*. Luxembourg: Eurostat.

Evers, A. and Leichsenring, K. (1994) Paying for informal care. *Ageing International*, March: 29–40.

Fell, S. and Foster, A. (1994) *Ages of Experience*. Glasgow: Scottish Consumer Council.

Florea, A., Columbini, L., Costanzo, A. and Cuneo, A. (1992) *Social and Economic Policies and Older People in Italy*. Rome: ISTISS.

Flynn, T. (1995) (ed.) *Solidarity Between Generations*. Quimper: Editions Nouvelles du Finistere.

Gallup (1992) *Results of Election Survey S4186 7–8 April*. London: Gallup.

Gaskin, K. and Davis Smith, J. (1995) *A New Civic Europe? A Study of the Extent and Role of Volunteering*. London: Volunteer Centre UK.

General Household Survey (GHS) (1987) *Supplement on Voluntary Work*. London: HMSO.

General Household Survey (GHS) (1994) *General Household Survey 1992*. London: HMSO.

Ginn, J. (1993) Grey power: age-based organisations' response to structured inequalities. *Critical Social Policy*, 38: 23–47.

Ginn, J. and Arber, S. (1995) 'Only connect': gender relations and ageing, in S. Arber and J. Ginn (eds) *Connecting Gender and Ageing: A Sociological Approach*. Buckingham: Open University Press.

Groves, D. (1992) Occupational pension provision and women's poverty in old age, in C. Glendinning and J. Millar (eds) *Women and Poverty in Britain: the 1990s*. London: Harvester Wheatsheaf.

Guillemard, A-M. (1993) Older workers and the labour market, in A. Walker, J. Alber and A-M. Guillemard (eds) *Older People in Europe: Social and Economic Policies*. Brussels: DG V, Commission of the European Communities.

Hastrup, B. (1995) Contribution to 'Managing volunteers; global concerns, local responses', *Ageing International*, September: 34–6.

Health and Personal Social Services Statistics for England (1993). London: HMSO.

Henwood, M. (1992) *Through a Glass Darkly: Community Care and Elderly People*. London: King's Fund Institute.

House of Commons (1991) *Hansard*, 16 December 1991, col. 88. London: HMSO.

House of Commons Health Committee (1991) *Public Expenditure on Health Matters*. London: HMSO.

Howe, A. (1993) Attitudes to ageing. *St Mark's Review*, spring: 3–11.

Income Data Services (IDS) (1986) *Income Data Services Study Number 595*. London: IDS.

International Social Security Association (ISSA) (1995) *Trends in Social Security No. 8*. Geneva: International Social Security Association.

Johnson, P., Conrad, C. and Thomson, D. (eds) (1989) *Workers versus Pensioners: Intergenerational Justice in an Ageing World*. Manchester: Manchester University Press

Jones, A. and Longstone, L. (1990) *A Survey of Restrictions on Job Centre Vacancies*. London: Department of Employment.

Kern, A. (1990) *Is TESCO a Positive Agent of Productive Ageing?* Geneva: WHO.

Kohli, M., Rein, M., Guillemard, A-M. and Gunsteren, H. (1991) *Time for Retirement – Comparative Studies of Early Exit from the Labour Force*. Cambridge: Cambridge University Press.

Kuty, O. (1993) The social integration of older people in Belgium, in A. Walker (ed.) *Older People in Europe: Social Integration*. Brussels: CEC.

Laczko, F. and Phillipson, C. (1991) Great Britain: the contradictions of early exit, in M. Kohli, M. Rein, A.M. Guillemard and H. Van Gunsteren (eds) *Time for Retirement*. Cambridge: Cambridge University Press.

Laslett, P. (1971) *The World We Have Lost*, (2nd edn). Cambridge: Cambridge University Press.

Laslett, P. (1987) The emergence of the third age. *Ageing and Society*, 7(2): 133–60.

Laslett, P. (1994) The third age, the fourth age and the future. *Ageing and Society*, 14(3): 436–48.

Lewis, M. and Butler, R. (1972) Why is women's lib ignoring older women? *Aging and Human Development*, 3: 223–31.

Maltby, T. (1994) *Women and Pensions in Britain and Hungary: A Cross-National and Comparative Case Study of Social Dependency*. Aldershot: Avebury.

Metcalf, H. and Thompson, M. (1990) *Older Workers: Employer's Attitudes and Practices*. Sussex: Institute for Manpower Studies.

Midwinter, E. (1991) *The British Gas Report on Attitudes to Ageing*. London: British Gas.

Miles, J. (1994) Slow progress: why a political framework is necessary for the evaluation of pensioners' campaigns. *Generations Review*, 4(1): 4–7.

Moore, J., Tilson, B. and Witting, G. (1994) *An International Overview of Employment Policies and Practices Towards Older Workers*, DEE Research Series No. 29. London: Department for Education and Employment.

Myles, J. and Quadagno, J. (eds) (1991) *States, Labor Markets and the Future of Old-Age Policy*. Philadelphia: Temple University Press.

Ogg, J. and Bennett, G. (1992) Elder abuse in Britain, *British Medical Journal*, 305: 998–9.

Organization for Economic Cooperation and Development (OECD) (1988) *Reforming Public Pensions*. Paris: OECD.

O'Shea, E. (1993) The social integration of older people in Belgium, in A. Walker (ed.) *Older People in Europe: Social Integration*. Brussels: CEC.

Penhale, B. (1993) Local authority guidelines and procedures, in McCreadie, Claudine (ed.) *Elder abuse: New Findings and Policy Guidelines*. Proceedings of an Ageing Update conference Canterbury Hall, University of London, 10 December 1992. London: Age Concern Institute of Gerontology at King's College.

Platz, M. (1989) *Gamle il eget hjem*, Bind 1: Levekår, Rapport 89:12. København: Socialforskningsinstituttet.

Platz, M. and Petersen, N.F. (1992) *Social and Economic Policies and Older People in Denmark: Report for EC Actions on Older People*. Copenhagen: Danish National Institute of Social Research.

Quintin, O. (1993) Introduction, in M. Ferrara (ed.) *The Evaluation of Social Policies: Experiences and Perspectives*. Pavia: University of Pavia.

Qureshi, H. and Walker, A. (1989) *The Caring Relationship*. London: Macmillan.

Rallings, C. and Thrasher, M. (1992) Essex man stays loyal and the older woman is won over. *The Sunday Times*, 12 April: 1, 14.

Reday-Mulvay, G. (1990) Work and retirement: future prospects for the baby boom generation. *The Geneva Papers*, 55: 100–13.

Room, G., *et al.* (1992) *Observatory on National Policies to Combat Social Exclusion*, second annual report. Brussels: CEC.

Rosenmayer, L. and Kockeis, E. (1963) Propositions for a sociological theory of ageing and the family. *International Social Services Journal*, 15(3): 410–26.

Scherman, K.G. (1995) Major changes in Sweden's pension system. *Ageing International*, June: 27–31.

Schuller, T. and Walker, A. (1990) *The Time of Our Life*. London: IPPR.

Sohngen, M. and Smith, R. (1978) Images of old age in poetry. *The Gerontologist*, 18(2): 181–6.

Sørensen, A. (1988) *Vore levekår i tal, 1976 of 1986*, mimeo stencil, unpublished. København.

Taverne, D. (1995) *The Pension Time Bomb in Europe*. London: Federal Trust.

Taylor, P. and Walker, A. (1991) *Too Old at 50*. London: Campaign for Work.

Taylor, P. and Walker, A. (1992) 'Employers policies and attitudes towards the employment of older people', mimeo, University of Sheffield.

Taylor, P. and Walker, A. (1995) Utilising older workers. *Employment Gazette*, April: 141–5.

Thursz, D., Nusberg, C. and Prather, J. (eds) (1995) *Empowering Older People*. London: Cassell.

Till, R. (1993) Ageing in literature, in P. Kaim-Caudle, J. Keithley and A. Mullender (eds) *Aspects of Ageing*. London: Whiting and Birch.

Tillsley, C. (1990) *The Impact of Age Upon Employment*. Coventry: University of Warwick.

Townsend, P. (1979) *Poverty in the United Kingdom*. Harmondsworth: Penguin.

Tunstall, J. (1996) *Old and Alone*. London: Routledge.

Walker, A. (1980) The social creation of poverty and dependency in old age. *Journal of Social Policy*, 9(1): 49–75.

Walker, A. (1981) Social policy, social administration and the social construction of welfare. *Sociology*, 5(2): 225–50.

Walker, A. (1982) The social consequences of early retirement. *Political Quarterly*, 53(1): 61–72.

Walker, A. (1985a) Early retirement: release or refuge from the labour market? *Quarterly Journal of Social Affairs*, 1(3): 211–29.

Walker, A. (1985b) *The Care Gap*. London: Local Government Information Service.

Walker, A. (1986) The politics of ageing in Britain, in C. Phillipson, M. Bernard and P. Strang (eds) *Dependency and Interdependency in Old Age*. London: Croom Helm.

Walker, A. (1990) The economic 'burden' of ageing and the prospect of intergenerational conflict. *Ageing and Society*, 10(4): 377–96.

Walker, A. (1992) The poor relation, poverty among older women, in C. Glendinning and J. Millar (eds) *Women and Poverty in Britain: The 1990s*. London: Harvester Wheatsheaf.

Walker, A. (1993a) *Age and Attitudes – Main Results from a Eurobarometer Survey*. Brussels: CEC.

Walker, A. (ed.) (1993b) *Older People in Europe: Social Integration*. Brussels: CEC.

Walker, A. (ed.) (1996) *The New Generational Contract*. London: University College London Press.

Walker, A. and Taylor, P. (1993) Ageism versus productive ageing: the challenge of age discrimination in the labor market, in S. Bass, F. Caro and Y-P. Chen (eds) *Achieving a Productive Ageing Society*, pp. 61–80. Westport, CT: Auburn House.

Walker, A. and Warren, L. (1996) *Changing Services for Older People*. Buckingham: Open University Press.

Walker, A., Guillemard, A-M. and Alber, J. (1991) *Social and Economic Policies and Older People*. Brussels: CEC.

Walker, A., Guillemard, A-M. and Alber, J. (1993) *Older People in Europe: Social and Economic Policies*. Brussels: CEC.

Webster, K. (ed.) (1992) *Behind the Statistics*. London: Eurolink Age.

Wells, C. and Mosley, R. (1995) *B&Q 'Life begins at 50'*. Eastleigh, Hants: B&Q.

Westergaard, J., Noble, I. and Walker, A. (1989) *After Redundancy*. Oxford: Polity Press.

Whelan, C. T. and Whelan, B. J. (1988) *The Transition to Retirement*. Dublin: Economic and Social Research Institute.

Whiteford, P. and Kennedy, S. (1995) *Incomes and Living Standards of Older People*, DSS Research Report No. 34. London: HMSO.

Whiting, G., Moore, J. and Tilson, B. (1995) Employment policies and practices towards older workers: an international overview. *Employment Gazette*, April: 147–52.

Widdecombe, A. (1995) *Hansard*, 23 May 1995, cols 812–18.

World Bank (1994) *Averting the Old Age Crisis: Policies to Protect the Old and Promote Growth*. Oxford: Oxford University Press.

Index

France *(cont'd)*
  employment of older workers, 70, 71, 72
  feelings of loneliness, 26
  fertility rates, 14
  financial situations, 54, 55, 56
  health and social care, 91, 92, 93, 94
  intergenerational contact, 28
  involvement in voluntary organizations, 24
  life expectancy, 13, 15
  living standards, 47
  male/female ratio, 11
  older people living alone, 13, 35
  pensions, 49, 60, 62
    adequacy of, 57, 58, 67
    and concessions, 64, 66
  percentage of older people, 10, 11
  and policies towards older people, 123, 124
  political activity, 112, 113, 118
  politics and the media, 111
  poverty rates, 50, 51
  religious activities, 23
  and retirement, 84, 85
  and the social contract, 32
  UTAs (universities of the third age), 115
friends, contacts with, 25, 26, 36

gardening, 23
Gaskin, K., 38, 40, 41
gender
  and care of older people, 96, 103
  and income inequality, 6, 44, 45, 46, 53
  and life expectancy, 13, 15
  and living alone, 13, 35
  male/female ratio in the population, 11
  and older workers, 69–72, 83
    in the United Kingdom, 75–6
  and suicide rates, 42
  and unemployment, 76–7
  see also men; women
Germany
  activities of older people, 23
  and age discrimination, 88
  attitudes to the ageing process, 20
  caring for older people, 101, 102, 104, 106, 107, 108
  clubs/associations for older people, 39
  contacts with family and friends, 25, 26
  early retirement, 73, 74

  education and older people, 115
  employment of older workers, 70, 71, 83
  feelings of loneliness, 26
  fertility rates, 14
  financial situations, 54, 55, 56
  former FRG and GDR, 67, 123
  health and social care, 91, 92, 93, 94
  hospice movement, 100
  intergenerational contact, 28
  life expectancy, 15
  naming older people, 17, 18
  pensions, 46, 60, 61, 62, 67
    adequacy of, 57, 58
    and concessions, 64, 65, 66
    gender inequalities, 44
  percentage of older people, 10, 11
  and policies towards older people, 123, 124
  political activity, 111, 112, 113, 114, 118
  politics and the media, 110
  poverty rates, 50
  residential care, 92
  and respect for older people, 19
  retirement, 84, 85
    age of, 72, 73
  and the social contract, 32
  social integration projects, 38
  telephones and older people, 41
  unemployment, 74
  unification of, 8
  voluntary organizations, 39
Ginn, J., 17, 44, 45, 116
golden age, as name for older people, 16, 18
GPs (general practitioners), 95, 96, 98
grandparents, role of, 36
Greece
  activities of older people, 23
  and age discrimination, 88
  and age segregation, 29–30
  and the ageing process, 20, 21
  caring for older people, 101, 102, 104, 106, 108
  contacts with family and friends, 25
  education, 115
  employment of older workers, 70, 71
  feelings of loneliness, 26
  fertility rates, 14
  financial situations, 54, 55, 56, 57
  health and social care, 92, 93, 94
  interest in social problems, 29